End of Days

End of Days

Predictions of the End From Ancient Sources

BY RICHARD J. HOOPER

SANCTUARY PUBLICATIONS

End of Days:
Predictions of the End from Ancient Sources

Cover and book design:
Jane Perini, Thunder Mountain Design & Communications
www.thundermountaindesign.com

Published by Sanctuary Publications, Inc.
P.O. Box 20697, Sedona, AZ 86341

ISBN 13: 978-0-9843754-3-1 ISBN 10: 0-97843754-3-0
LCCN: 2011901810

For Eleanor and Woody

For all that you are and all that you've done.

May your days be filled with happiness.

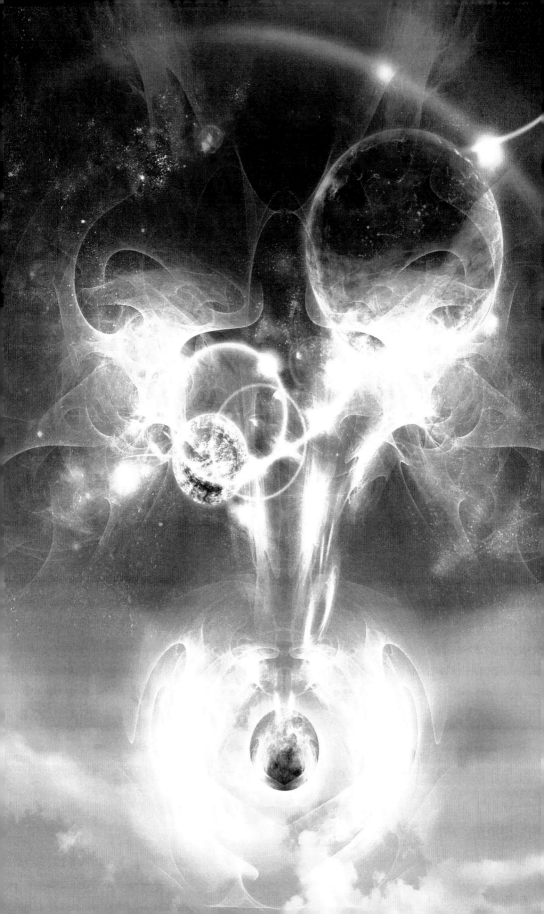

Man did not weave the web of life,
he is merely a strand in it.
Whatever he does to the web,
he does to himself.

- CHIEF SEATTLE

The Earth is degenerating today.
Bribery and corruption abound.
Children no longer obey their parents.
Every man wants to write a book.
It is evident that the end of the
world is fast approaching.

- ASSYRIAN TABLET—2800 B.C.E.

There are always those who'd like to
turn out the lights. So far we've been lucky.
They've always just been shy of a majority.

- DEAN KOONTZ

Contents

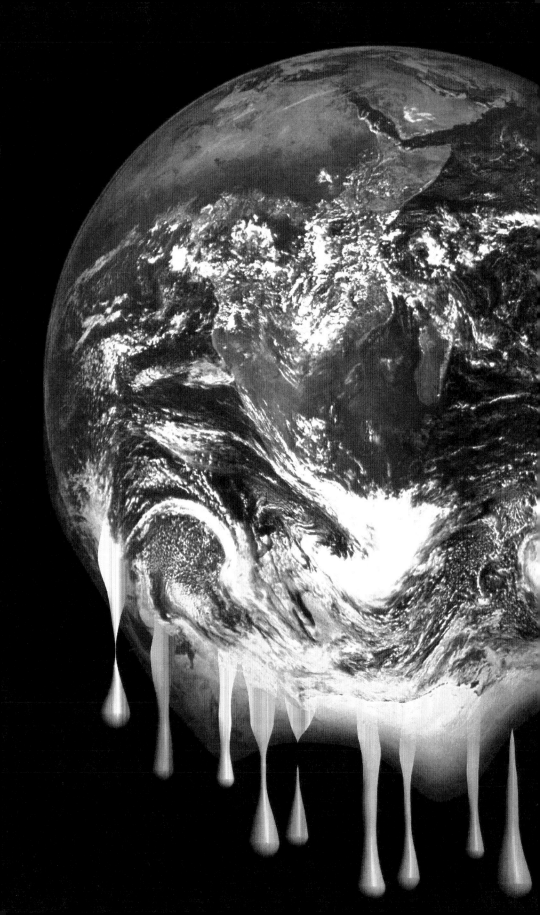

PROLOGUE

I Am Become Death, Destroyer of Worlds.

- J. ROBERT OPPENHEIMER,

INSPIRED BY THE *BHAGAVAD GITA* 14:3

Kali Yuga, 9,000,000,000 C.E.

Looking somewhat like a bulked-up, armored, version of an ancient cockroach, the luminescent hard-shelled insect could not move. Retreat into the once cold waters of the cave pools was now impossible because those waters were now boiling.

The aquatic insect couldn't move anyway; its feet were melding with the rock, as the rock became oozing magma. As the last of its species—as the last of all species—the creature sensed that its life had come to an end.

Other insects had adapted to cave life over millions of years as the planet began to heat up. Having lived in total darkness for millennia these creatures needed no eyes. They negotiated rock walls and cold water pools through the use of other senses, but none of that mattered now. The springs and deeply hidden pools within the bowels of Earth were burning up in the steam of evaporation.

Conditions on the surface of the planet were far worse. Clouds had not existed for millions of years, so it never rained. Waterfalls, rivers and lakes had dried up long ago, and even the

great seas that had once covered the Earth were now lifeless dunes of sand, and even the sand was melting. The solar radiation produced by the "red giant" that engulfed Earth had blasted away the hydrogen from all water on the surface of the planet. The oceans had become molten—just as they had been in the dawn of creation.

Had there been any life forms to witness conditions on the surface of Earth, they would not see a blue sky during the day, or stars at night, because night no longer existed. All living creature would see only a giant inferno that overwhelmed Earth. This red giant had once been Earth's sun and the star of this particular solar system. Now it had become Kali, the goddess of death and destruction.

Although it was dying, the sun was very hungry. As it had grown in size, it had engulfed Mercury, then Venus, and had now expanded beyond Earth's equator. Even so, it would be millions of years before it moved on to devour Mars. Before Kali was finished, she might devour the entire solar system.

Sol had turned into this monster of fire once it had burned up all of its hydrogen fuel. It would continue to expand for many millions of years before the fire eventually burned itself out. When that happened, what had once been the life-giving source of Earth- would collapse into a "white dwarf" the size of Earth itself.

Just as the sun and the red giant would not exist forever, the white dwarf, too, would one day die. If its density at that time was great enough, it could rip a hole in the fabric of space and become a singularity—a black hole in space. Even if this didn't happen, it would eventually be caught in the gravitational pull of some other marauding black hole.

Death and destruction also awaited the galaxy that Earth- lings had once called the Milky Way. Death was the destiny of the Universe itself. In the end there would be only darkness and silence in vast space.

Kali looked upon her destruction and saw that it was good, for such is the natural way of never ending change. Worlds come; worlds go. Creation is always followed by destruction. Planets, galaxies and universes are born. Planets, galaxies and universes die. That is the way of things. That is the dance of Shiva, whose purpose it is to grind existence into non-existence. In the end, all we are is dust in the wind.

On the eve of destruction, the Earth died screaming.

Kali Yuga 2112 C.E.

The message came through to the captain and crew of the enormous space freighter just after it had broken out of Earth's gravitational pull. Everyone knew the message was coming and nobody wanted to hear it. Everyone on board already knew what the President of the World Federation of States would say to them. What else could he say?

On Earth, twenty-five million more human beings awaited the ominous bon voyage.

The captain of the freighter—an old salt the crew called Rusty for his mess of unruly red hair and beard—wasn't anxious to hear the words, and even though he was getting paid for this run, he wished he'd never accepted the job. His orders were to fly to Mars, enter its orbit and remain there indefinitely. Indefinitely! No one on board knew if or when they would see Earth again, not that it really mattered.

Most of all, the captain had a bad feeling about his cargo. Attached to the bow of the ship was the most unlikely of things: an enormous geodesic dome more than half a mile in diameter. Two more domes of equal size were connected to the freighter—one just starboard of the bow, and the other portside.

The captain felt the burden of responsibility weigh him down as if it were an asteroid made of lead. He was a good-hearted soul, and his crew would confirm that. But he could hardly bear all the hopes and dreams of humanity. The huge domes attached to the freighter were actually greenhouses, and the treasure they contained were Earth's last forests.

The com whistle blew to alert captain and crew of the incoming message. Familiar as it was, the whistle gave the captain a start and made him grimace. The crew stopped what they were doing and all turned toward the speakers. The gardeners in the domes put down their tools and bowed their heads as the voice of the President delivered the fateful announcement:

"On this day we humbly beg forgiveness for our great sins. We dedicate these last forests of our once beautiful world, and we hope and pray that they will one day be able to return to our fouled planet and create life anew. Until that day, May God bless these forests, and the brave men who care for them."

Weeks passed, then months. The crew became demoralized, and Captain Rusty turned to the comfort of the bottle. Among the ship's personnel, only the gardeners were engaged and happy. To them, the forests were cathedrals, and they the priests—dispensing the sacraments of light, water and nutrients. They considered their work a sacred duty, and not one of them was prepared for the message that finally reached the ship from Earth. The voice of the freighter's captain filled the domes like poison gas:

"Ahoy. We have just received orders to abandon the domes. Once they are far from the ship, we are to destroy the forests with nuclear detonations and return our ship to commercial service. I have received no explanation . . . May God have mercy on us all."

Fields of children running wild
in the sun.
Like a forest is your child, growing wild
in the sun.
Doomed in his innocence
in the sun.

Gather your children by your side,
in the sun.
Tell them all their love will die,
Tell them why
in the sun.

Tell them it's not too late,
Cultivate, one by one
Tell them to harvest and rejoice
in the sun.

- JOAN BAEZ—FROM THE MOVIE, "SILENT RUNNING"

INTRODUCTION

*Ours is not a perfect world, and therefore the old must
die in order that the young, that which is more perfect
or at any rate capable of greater perfection, may live.
Thus death becomes a thing necessary and useful in the
evolution of the whole. The destruction of one celestial
body contributes to the progress of the rest of the universe.*

- MAX WILHELM MEYER

The word, *eschatology*, comes from two Greek words: *eschaton*, meaning "the end" and logos, meaning "word" or "words about." Eschatology, then, is the study of, or theology about, the end of the world or, more precisely, the end of the world *as we know it*.

The Buddha's sermon on the actual end of planet Earth counts as eschatological literature, but most religious eschatological texts are not concerned with the eventual demise of our planet. Most eschatological literature is "apocalyptic," and has to do with planetary chaos and the complete collapse of human civilization.

Apocalyptic literature is rarely just about destruction, however. It is also about creation—the creation of a "new" world that will follow the destruction of the present one. The Greek word, apocalypse, literally means "revelation," but in the Judeo-Christianity the word came to mean "revelations about the end of the world."

The apocalyptic thesis is this: since humanity has been unable or unwilling either to cooperate with the natural order or to live by God's laws, we ourselves are responsible for creating a world full of evil, hate, greed, war and injustice. Add to this the belief that this world—and the entire Universe—is also under the dominion of a personified evil force which opposes God and the divine order of things.

In the beginning, our world was perfect, but now it is permanently flawed. We have no power—but less the will—to change for the better, so it must be destroyed and replaced with a new world in which evil does not exist. The beginning of the destructive phase will be announced by the arrival of a messiah figure who will lead the forces of good in a battle against the forces of evil.

After a period of destruction and great violence, the forces of good will win the war, and after this happens all of humanity will be judged. Those who have done evil during their lives will be punished and/or exterminated, while those who have done good in life will be rewarded with eternal life in a brand new world in which evil—even the *possibility* of evil—has been banished forever.

This apocalyptic drama—destruction, cosmic warfare, the coming of a messiah, the judgment of humanity and the ushering in of a new world sounds like the drama that takes place in the *New Testament's* book of *Revelation*. But an almost identical story can be found in the sacred texts of Zoroastrians, Jews, Muslims, Hindus, and Buddhists.

For religions like Hinduism and Buddhism, however, creation, destruction and a new creation, is a cyclical process that happens over and over again throughout the existence of the Universe. It has been going on since the beginning of time, and it will continue until the end of time. Believing that all things are impermanent, Hindus and Buddhists see these cycles as inevitable and natural, while Jews, Christians and Muslims believe that creation, destruction, and re-creation are one time events.

The end of the present world—as we know it—has been pre-

dicted for at least 3,000 years, and we might wonder why this is so. Only in our own times has humanity faced world-ending scenarios: total economic collapse, global warming, dying oceans, mass extinction of species, deforestation, uncontrolled population growth, terrorism and the ever present threat of nuclear annihilation. Any one of the threats that face us could destroy the world as we know it, and imagining the end requires no prophetic abilities. But such threats did not exist in antiquity, so why did the ancients believe their world was going to end?

The literary genre of apocalyptic in Judeo-Christianity was a response to specific historical events. Apocalyptic literature came into being around 200 B.C.E., and ceased to exist after 200 C.E. During this four-hundred year period Jews and Christians not only believed that the world was about to end, but that it would end at any moment. If these ancients didn't face the historical stressors we do, they must have faced a lengthy period of time when life seemed unbearable.

Jews, Christians and Muslims all believed—and many still believe—that the world is an impossibly evil place. It is impossible for human beings to make this world better, so redemption can come only as a result of divine intervention. God must break into history, send a messiah, and wage war against evil until it is completely vanquished.

The master apocalyptic story also tells us that this is not just a local problem; evil rules throughout the Universe. There is an evil force in this Universe with a power that is almost, but not quite, equal to God's. The Apocalypse, by necessity, will be cosmos-wide war—the ultimate and final battle between all good and all evil in the Universe.

Hindus and Buddhists believe in good and evil, but consider these opposites as two sides of the same reality. In a Universe made up of polarities, pairs of opposites balance each other. The Taoist symbol of Yin and Yang is a visual representation of this perfect balance.

Since this understanding of how the Universe works is common to all Eastern philosophy, one would not expect to find the apocalyptic myth in the literature of these religions. And yet the classic myth does exist in Hindu and Buddhist literature, even if it is found only in relatively obscure texts. Hindus and Buddhists never produced apocalyptic literature in the classic sense.

One of the things that makes Judeo-Christian apocalypses distinct in the history of literature is the extensive use of esoteric symbolism, fantastic beasts, occult numbers and obscure names. None of these literary elements of apocalyptic literature was esoteric or confusing to their intended audiences. Most modern readers, however, no longer understand the historical and biblical context of this literature, and tend to supply their own meaning to this coded language.

Apocalypses were, in fact, written in code, but not the kind of code most people imagine. To understand the language of apocalyptic one must be thoroughly familiar with the historical context in which they were written, and be thoroughly steeped in the imagery and meaning of biblical language used in books like *Daniel* and *Ezekiel*, and extra-canonical texts such as *First* and *Second Enoch.*

If the modern reader lacks points of reference, so did the apocalyptic author's enemies. And this was precisely the point. Apocalypses were written in code so that they would be understood only by the audiences to whom they were specifically addressed.

Apocalypses were written to convey important news and information. They were also written for the purpose of encouraging faith in times of extreme oppression and persecution. It is very important to understand that apocalypses were not meant to be understood as predictions of future events. They all referred to historical events taking place at the time of their writing! As the Biblical scholar, David Barr, writes in his book, *Tales of the End*, "Apocalypses don't mean what they say; they mean what they mean."

Hindus and Buddhists did not produce apocalyptic literature because they had no reason to believe the end of the world was imminent. For them, the drama would take place at a predetermined time, and there was nothing one needed to do to prepare for the inevitable. Just when such events will take place is of little interest because Hindus and Buddhists try to live their lives in the present moment.

In Hinduism, the span of time between the creation and destruction of the world as we know it—as well as the creation and destruction of the Earth and the Universe—is determined by the individual length of each of four cycles of time known as *Yugas* or *Kalpas*. The last of the four *Yugas* or ages, the *Kali Yuga*—so named for *Kali*, goddess of destruction—began long before recorded history. When Homo sapiens first appeared on Earth, the *Kali Yuga* had already begun.

The Buddhist system of *Kalpas* is very close to the Hindu

system of *Yugas*, and is also divided into four epochs, aeons or ages of Earth history. The first age was seen to be the golden age of perfection. From then on, each age became shorter in duration and increasingly degenerative. The fourth, and final, age signaled a time of extreme and rapid deterioration and destruction on a vast scale.

While eschatology in the Christian sense has never been of primary interest in Eastern religions, all people realize sooner or later that nothing can remain the same forever. All things are impermanent. Destruction always follows creation, for that is the law of the Universe. The apparent struggle between good and evil in this world is not only natural and inevitable, it is a balancing act that will continue to the end of time.

For Jews and Christians, the Apocalypse and the new world to come, meant the end of human suffering. All human beings desire to escape the suffering inherent in this world, but the Abrahamic religions look to a supernatural world for salvation, while Hindus and Buddhists look to themselves.

The Hindu and Buddhist religions teach that if we want to

get off the wheel of *Samsara*—the endless cycle of birth, death and rebirth that inevitably brings us back into the world of suffering—then we must change the way we perceive reality. Suffering ends the moment we become aware that it is nothing more than a projection of one's own discriminating mind. Shakespeare's Hamlet said it best: "There is nothing good or bad, but thinking makes it so."

If we were "enlightened," Hindus and Buddhists tell us, we would suddenly see the world in a different way altogether. We would still perceive polarities, but we would realize that they have no ultimate reality. We would realize that everything in the material world is, in a sense, illusory. Things "exist," but only to the extent that our minds experience them. Change the mind—seek out and find its true nature, and polarities cease to exist for all practical purposes.

Such a philosophy would have seemed meaningless to those Jews and Christians who suffered under oppression and persecution during the historical period in which apocalypses were written. For Jews, apocalypses were a response to what they considered the unbearable yoke of foreign occupation. Their history began in slavery. After escaping Egypt and capturing a land of their own, there were precious few periods of history when Jews were a free and self-determined people. The ancient Israelites were conquered repeatedly; first by the Babylonians, then the Assyrians, the Greeks, and finally the Romans.

Apocalyptic literature became a way of voicing Jewish frustration with their people's lot in life. The Jews rebelled again and again, sometimes shaking off the grip of their oppressors—but only to fall victims to the next empire de jour. It had happened so many times, that by the second century B.C.E., Jewish theologians began to believe that they would never be a free people in this world if God Himself did not intervene. Considering themselves to be God's chosen people, they believed that God surely wouldn't allow their suffering to continue forever. What no doubt began as only a hope, eventually became messianic expectation—a Jewish mindset that reached its peak in the time of Jesus. Unfortunately, this expectation was dashed as well.

When the Jews rebelled against Roman occupation in 66 C.E., Rome's legions responded with maximum force. Thousands of Jews were crucified daily. Under the leadership of Titus, Roman legions utterly destroyed the sacred city of Jerusalem and the second Temple in 70 C.E. The Temple was the center, and very essence, of Jewish religious life. When it became nothing more than rubble, the majority of Jews in the southern kingdom of Judah fled their homeland in the first great Jewish Diaspora, scattering to the four winds. Three years later, the last stronghold of Jewish resistance at Masada was crushed.

Yet, even in the Diaspora, the Jews rebelled throughout Mesopotamia. Sixty-two years after the destruction of Jerusalem, a second revolt began under the leadership of Bar-Kokhba. Jewish troops retook Jerusalem and reestablished a Jewish state for a brief time, but their revolt was crushed by the emperor Hadrian's own elite legions.

Jewish presence in the Holy Land mostly ended after this last defeat, and over time many Jews began to give up on the idea that the Messiah was going to come anytime soon. In the Diaspora, rabbinical Judaism—the Pharisaism of Jesus' day—became the norm, and apocalypticism gradually became irrelevant.

As for Christians, when the Roman Empire finally grew tired of persecuting them, apocalyptic literature no longer served any useful purpose either. By 200 C.E., the literary genre of apocalyptic ceased to exist.

Eastern and "Western" religions have always looked at the world quite differently. Hindus and Buddhists see human history as relatively unimportant, while Jews, Christians and Muslims look for ultimate meaning and purpose in life. Life is a serious affair for the religions of the Middle East, but for Hindus and

Buddhists life's dramas are little more than what Hindus call *Lila*, or the "creative play" of Brahman, the Absolute. To pass eternity, That-Which-Is—the undifferentiated one—creates and destroys one universe after another for sheer amusement and entertainment. In manifesting endless universes, worlds and individual beings, the One chooses to forget that It is One and pretends to be the many.

These worlds and universes are the stages upon which *That-Which-Is* produces and directs all manner of complex dramas—comedies and tragedies alike. We, the actors upon the stage, unaware that we are the One, take our parts seriously, thinking them to be real. We believe that we built the stage upon which we act, not realizing that we are only dreaming it into existence. We fool ourselves into believing the unreal is real because the alternative is too frightening to contemplate: *I* am both the dream and the dreamer. There is no "other."

Through endless cycles of creation and destruction, That-Which-Is plays hide and seek with Itself. It allows Itself to forget It's true nature. It chooses to fall asleep and dream that it is not One, but many. The play must go on. The curtain must rise, and the actors must play their parts. *Brahman* breathes out and a universe comes into being; Brahman breaths in and a universe ceases to be.

Because universes and worlds are created and destroyed time after time, Hindus and Buddhists think of "time" as cyclical, not linear. For the Abrahamic faiths—Judaism, Christianity and Islam—however, there is only one universe, and time is a linear progression from creation to destruction.

It might be more accurate, however, to say that Judaism, Christianity and Islam believe in two worlds, not one. There is the heavenly realm in which God and his heavenly host dwell, and there is this mundane world that God created for us lesser creatures.

Since God cannot make mistakes, He created a perfect world at the beginning of time. But forces outside of Himself corrupted

it. A second force appeared in the Universe, and it opposed God, causing even His finest creation—humanity—to rebel against Him. This world has been under the dominion of the Evil One for a very long time, but Satan's rule will not last forever. Eventually, God will set things straight by destroying His enemy and once again create a perfect world. This new world will be free of all defects—even the possibility of evil. Sin, greed, hate, war, injustice, sickness and death will be banished forever.

Judaism, Christianity and Islam weren't the only religions which imagined an extreme makeover of the present world. Neither did these religions originate the idea. The end of the present world, and the ushering in of a new world, is an archetypal myth first found in the religious texts of Zoroastrianism, the religion of ancient Persia (modern day Iran), vestiges of which still remain.

From there, the apocalyptic myth seems to have been exported to other lands and religions. Jews adopted the myth of radical dualism from Zoroastrians, and Christians and Muslims adopted it from Judaism. It is possible that the Aryan people of Persia migrated to India and brought the myth with them. If that was the case, then Buddhism—which originated in India—borrowed the apocalyptic myth from Hinduism.

However the story of the end of the world came about, to think of it only in the negative sense of destruction would be to miss the point. Eschatology, correctly understood, is ultimately about hope for the future, and hope for the perfection of humanity. This higher vision of ourselves—this universal longing for our species to advance toward the light seems to be permanently encoded in our DNA.

Negativity is not the essential nature of man. We need only go to the movies or read novels to know that the good guys must always win, and justice must always prevail. The audience insists on a happy ending to every story. Of course justice doesn't always prevail in reality, the good guys don't always win, and we don't live happily ever after. But we have set a high standard for human behavior, and I think that it tells us something positive about human nature.

Humanity—for all of its stupidity, greed, lust and avarice—still looks toward the future with an attitude of affirmation, not negation. We may be apathetic, but we still dream of a world where evil, sickness and death have been vanquished, and where all things work together for the good.

For such a world to come into being, we must first confront the polarity of natures within ourselves, both personally and as a species. As human beings, we are all capable of both good and evil. Denying our nature is counterproductive. Modern psychologists encourage us instead to embrace our "shadow," our dark side, for only then will we understand why we do what we do.

Only then can we be made whole again. We must become one with ourselves before we can become one with God.

Though the world is full of people who seem to want nothing more than to destroy, there are far more of us who seek to create and perfect. Only human apathy keeps us from creating the world that the biblical prophet, Isaiah, imagined long ago—a world in which swords would be turned into plowshares and lions would lie down with lambs.

John Lennon dared to imagine a world without formal religions and the strife they cause, a world where greed and hunger no longer exist—but is replaced by a brotherhood of man, living life in peace. This is the perennial dream.

The great Catholic theologian and mystic, Pierre Teilhard de Chardin, describes the "end of the world" in his book, *The Future of Man:*

> When the end of time is at hand, a terrifying spiritual pressure will be exerted on the confines of the real, built up by the desperate efforts of the souls tense with longing to escape from the earth. This pressure will be unanimous. . . It is then, we may be sure, that the Parousia will be realized in a creation that has been taken to the climax of its capacity for union. The single act of assimilation and synthesis that has been going on since the beginning of time will then at last be made plain . . . The trumpets of the angels are but a poor symbol. It will be impelled by the most powerful organic attraction that can be conceived (the very force by which the universe holds together) that the monads will join in a headlong rush to the place irrevocably appointed for them by the total adulthood of things and the inexorable irreversibility of the whole history of the world . . . Like a vast tide, Being will have engulfed the shifting sands of

being. Within a now tranquil ocean, each drop of which, nevertheless, will be conscious of remaining itself, the astonishing adventure of the world will have ended. The dream of every mystic, the eternal pantheist ideal, will have found its full and legitimate satisfaction. *'Erit in omnibus omnia Deus.'*

If the world is an evil place, it is not *inherently* evil. It was created perfect, and only our misguided attempts to change its nature have caused us problems. If, as a species, we were to become more intelligent and less destructive, perhaps we could re-enter Eden. The apocalyptic myth, however, does not allow for a "velvet revolution." The world's eschatological literature suggests that change can be brought about only by extreme violence. The armies of God will be taking no prisoners. But we could also choose not to believe this myth.

If we were able to see the world with new eyes we would realize that this war between good and evil must be fought and won . . . within ourselves. Jesus taught that the Kingdom of God is already present—that we should not look for it in the sky, beneath the sea, or in the future. We do not need to change the world and we do not need a new world. What we need is to be able to perceive the world, and ourselves, differently. The positive transformation of the world must begin with the transformation of our own consciousness.

We experience ourselves, our thoughts and feelings as something separate from the rest. A kind of optical delusion of consciousness. This delusion is a kind of prison for us, restricting us to our personal desires and to affection for a few persons nearest to us. Our task must be to free ourselves from the prison by widening our circle of compassion to embrace all living creatures

and the whole of nature in its beauty. The true value of a human being is determined by the measure and the sense in which they have obtained liberation from the self. We shall require a substantially new manner of thinking if humanity is to survive.

- ALBERT EINSTEIN

I. Common Themes in Eschatological Traditions

The people liked the prospect of the end of the world because it would be a spectacle, something to relieve the fearful monotony of their lives. Funerals and weddings were commonplace, and nothing could have been so interesting to them as the coming of the end of the world . . . unless it had been a first-class circus.

- EDWARD EGGLESTON

J t is rather surprising to discover that even in Hindu and Buddhist mythology we find the theme of vengeance as essential to the story of a final cosmic battle. In the Buddhist *Kalachakra Tantra* text, borrowing images from the Hindu *Vishnu Puranas*, we even find predictions of a Buddhist holy war against Islam—even a war between Hindus and Buddhists!

This seems impossible, but the literature exists. Cosmic warfare, final judgment, the casting of sinners into a fiery hell—one does not think of such negatives in relationship to the teachings of Hinduism and Buddhism, but they seem to be universal.

All traditions also share the belief in the decline of morality, the eclipse of *dharma* teachings and the end of civilization as we know it. If there is something better to come, the literature insists that it will come only after much blood has been spilled.

The New Age movement is predicting a quantum leap of

human consciousness as the ultimate result of our current planetary crises. One would like to believe this, but it is rather hard to imagine given our present circumstances. Destruction seems likely, but perhaps destruction is necessary.

All eschatological myths insist that this destruction will be signaled by the arrival of an Avatar—an incarnation or agent of God. The ancient Zoroastrians waited for *Saoshyant.* Aztecs and Mayans predicted the coming of *Quetzalcoatl.* Jews expect the Messiah. Christians believe that Christ will return to Earth. Sunni Muslims await *Muntazar.* Shiite Muslims look for the *Mahdi,* and Sufi Muslims predict the coming of *Khidr.* Buddhists look for the Maitreya Buddha, and the *Amida Buddha,* The Hindus wait for *Kalki* or *Javada.*

The Hindu avatar, Krishna, speaking as Immortal Being Itself states in the *Bhagavad Gita*:

> Whenever there is decay of righteousness . . . and there is exaltation or unrighteousness, then I Myself come forth . . . for the destruction of evil-doers, for the sake of firmly establishing righteousness, I am born from age to age.

> - *BHAGAVAD GITA* 4:7-8

An untitled Gnostic-Christian text states:

> So when he had seen the grace with which the hidden Father had endowed him, he himself desired to lead back the universe to the hidden Father, for the Father's will is this: that the universe should return to him.

There is commonality between traditions having to do with ages of time as well.

Hinduism divided time in four ages: the *Satya-Yuga* (1,728,000 years), *Treta-Yuga* (1,296,000 years), *Dvapala-Yuga* (864,000 years) and the *Kali-Yuga* (432,000 years.)

Buddhism also divided history into four periods, or *Kalpas*: the *Ayu-Kalpa, Antah-Kalpa, Asankya-Kalpa*, and *Maha-Kalpa*. Even Zoroastrianism posited four ages, each lasting 3,000 years. As for cycles of time, Gnostics used the *Ouroborus*, the symbol of a serpent swallowing its own tail, to suggest the endless cycles of eternity—which is also suggested in the *yin-yang* symbol of the *Tao* in Taoism.

Even within the framework of linear time found in the Abrahamic faiths, there is a sense of "ages" in history. Jesus, in the *Gospel of Matthew*, commented that we were living at the end of an age. Whether time is linear or cyclical, all belief systems agree that Earth history is entropic. It begins with a golden age and gradually degenerates into a final age of chaos, misery and destruction. Following from the second law of thermodynamics, entropy means that order in a closed system always decreases, and that this process is irreversible. Destruction is inevitable, and what is inevitable should simply be accepted.

II. The Cosmic Drama in Eastern Philosophy

There is neither creation nor destruction,
neither destiny nor free will,
neither path nor achievement;
this is the final truth.

- SRI RAMANA MAHARSHI

To explain how the Universe worked, ancient Hindu philosophers conceived of *Brahman*—Ultimate Reality—as the trinitarian godhead consisting of *Brahma*, the Creator, *Vishnu* the Sustainer, and *Shiva* the Destroyer. All things exist within Ultimate Reality, so creation and destruction—like all pairs of opposites—are inseparable. One cannot exist without the other. Creation has within it the seeds of destruction, and vice versa. All perceived dualities are merely two sides of the same coin. In Taoism, the *Tao* cannot exist without both of its component parts: yin and yang. In Eastern philosophy, all things are interconnected and inseparable.

Hindus tell us that we live in the *Kali-Yuga*, the fourth and final age of this particular cosmic cycle. This age is ruled by Kali, goddess of death and destruction who devours all forms.

Kali is the "consort" of *Shiva* in his *kala*, or black, aspect. Like *Krishna*, *Kali* is also time and death. As *Shakti* (power) *Kali* also represents the goddess of all those who have killed their material desires and want only supreme consciousness in the lap of the Ultimate Mother.

The Buddha's division of four ages include formation, existence, degeneration and destruction. Upon destruction, all things return to their base elements. After a long time, the elements group together again and a new process of creation begins. The Universal cosmic cycles have no beginning and no end. Time has no meaning in this system, as all is cyclical.

Many early Gnostic Christians had this same perception and understanding of the nature of reality. In The *Gospel of Mary* (Magdalene) Jesus' disciples ask him about the nature of matter—whether it will be destroyed or not—and he replies: "Every nature, every modeled form, every creature, exists in and with each other. They will dissolve again into their own proper root [origin]. For the nature of matter is dissolved into what belongs to its nature." And in *The Gospel of Thomas* Jesus says: "This heaven will pass away and that which is above it will pass away."

III. Was Jesus an Apocalyptic Preacher?

Let us pardon him his hope of a vain apocalypse,
and of a second coming in great triumph upon the
clouds of heaven. Perhaps these were errors of others
rather than his own; and if it be true that he himself
shattered the general illusion, what matters it, since his
dream rendered him strong against death, and
sustained him in a struggle to which he might
otherwise have been unequal?

- ERNEST RENAN

The author of *Revelation* believed that the end of the world was at hand. The apostle, Paul, before him believed the same thing, as did John the Baptist before him. There are many sayings attributed to Jesus in the canonical Gospels that seem to suggest that Jesus agreed with these men. But many modern scholars believe that virtually all of these attributions are not historical. They believe that these words were put into Jesus' mouth by the later Christian evangelists who wrote the canonical Gospels.

John the Baptist was a contemporary of Jesus, and Jesus likely associated with him in some manner, perhaps as a disciple. If that was the case, then some scholars believe that Jesus may have left the Baptist's community over a disagreement about the issue of the apocalypse.

Certainly John the Baptist believed in the coming of a new world, and his mission was to tell others that they needed to be ready for the end by repenting of their sins, and sinning no more. Paul also believed in a new world to come and preached endlessly on the subject of repentance. For both of these men, anyone who was not prepared for what was about to happen would be cast into the outer regions. The question is, did Jesus believe any of this? If he did, then he would have been as wrong as John and Paul. None of us like the idea of Jesus being wrong about anything.

In the *Gospel of Luke*, the Pharisees ask Jesus when the kingdom of God is going to come, and Jesus responds that "The kingdom of God does not come in such a way as to be seen. No one will say, 'Look, here it is,' or 'There it is!' because the kingdom of God is within you." Some scholars argue that the better translation of the Greek word, *entos*, should be "in your midst" rather than "within." But that is not the case where this saying appears in the *Gospel of Thomas* (two versions), in *Dialog of the Savior* and in the *Gospel of Mary* (Magdalene). These two gospels were written later than *Luke*, but the *Gospel of Thomas* versions predate Luke's version, perhaps by as much as fifty years. So it seems likely that this saying can be attributed to the historical Jesus.

In Matthew's Gospel, as well as in *Luke* and *Mark*, Jesus called the kingdom a "mystery." And again in the *Gospel of John*, Jesus says that no one can see the kingdom without being born anew—that is, be able to see reality directly, without conditioning, as would be the case for an infant. In all of these cases, Jesus talks about the kingdom as a present reality—most likely a reality that has always existed.

Add to all of this the fact that in the two "source" gospels, the *Gospel of Thomas* and in the earliest layer of the Gospel of "Q" (a gospel that once existed, but can now only be found embedded within the Gospels of *Matthew* and *Luke*), Jesus makes no apocalyptic utterances of any kind. These early collections of Jesus' sayings predate the earliest narrative Gospel, that of *Mark*, by twenty years! Both were written around 50 C.E., whereas Mark wasn't written until 70 C.E.

Many scholars, therefore, believe that apocalypticism and eschatological preaching were not original to Jesus and his disciples, but only later crept into Christianity when many of John the Baptist's disciples joined the Jesus movement after John was beheaded.

In the *Gospel of Thomas*, Jesus is asked by his disciples, "Tell us how our end will come." Jesus gives a Zen-like answer: "Have you discovered the beginning, that you search for the end? In the place where the beginning is, there the end will be. Blessed is he who will stand at the beginning: He will know the end and will not taste death."

IV. Vengeance as an Eschatological Theme

He who seeks vengeance just digs two graves:
one for his enemy and one for himself.

- CHINESE PROVERB

One thing that Jewish, Christian and Muslim eschatology have in common is vengeance. Christians believe only they will survive. For Jews, most other nations will be wiped out. For Muslims, only those who convert to Islam will be spared, while the Madhi and his armies will exterminate every other person on Earth.

Written a century before the time of Jesus, the Qumran War Scroll speaks of the "Day of Vengeance." On this day there will be "everlasting destruction for all the company of Belial [all heretics] and of the *Kittim* [Romans] there will be no remnant left."

The author continues,

On the trumpets of battle formations they shall write, *For the Divisions of God for the Vengeance of His Wrath on the Sons of Darkness.*

. . . On the trumpets of massacre they shall write, *The Mighty Hand of God in War shall Cause all the Ungodly Slain to Fall . . .*

. . . God has smitten all the sons of darkness; His fury shall not end until they are utterly consumed . . . On their standards shall be written, *War of God, Vengeance of God, Trial of God, Reward of God, Power of God, Retributions of God, Might of God, Extermination of God for all the Nations of Vanity* . . . The priests shall continue to blow the trumpets of Massacre. The holy will anoint themselves with the blood of nations of vanity.

In the *Revelation* of John, the author revels in God's punishment of the enemy: ". . . and he shall be tormented with fire and sulphur in the presence of the holy angels and in the presence of the Lamb. And the smoke of their torment goes up for ever and ever; and they have no rest, day or night, these worshipers of the beast and its image . . . " ". . . Foul and evil sores came upon the men," and they had only blood to drink. "Men were scorched by fierce heat. . . gnawed their tongues in anguish." And great hailstones, heavy as a hundred-weight, dropped on men." Those who worshipped the Beast, "were thrown alive into the lake of fire . . . and the rest were slain by the sword . . . Those whose names were not written in the Book of Life would be thrown into the lake of fire. In the end, only 144,000 of the elect will be saved, while all others would be cast into the fiery pit.

This Christian God would even wreak His vengeance upon nature:

The second angel poured his bowl into the sea, and it became like the blood of a dead man, and every living thing died that was in the sea. The third angel poured his bowl into the rivers and the fountains of water, and they became blood.

- *REVELATION* 16:3-4

As for Islam, it is actually a living apocalyptic religion, and declared itself as such at the very beginning. *Allah* declared his wrath against enemies of Islam in the words of Mohammed:

> Behold, God sent me with a sword just before the hour
> [of judgment] and placed my daily sustenance beneath
> the shadow of my spear, and humiliation and contempt
> on those who oppose me.

Islam has always been spread by the sword, and just before he died, Mohammed told his followers that they must conquer the entire world in the next one hundred years. Jihad, holy war, is the way of Islam and if many Muslims don't really believe in the violence that is the central core of Islam, it is only because they choose to ignore the teachings of their prophet in *The Koran*. *The Koran* is clear on the subject of Muslims ruling the world.

V. The End of Days
in Zoroastrianism

I shall tell you a great secret, my friend.
Do not wait for the last judgment, it takes place every day.

- ALBERT CAMUS

J udaism was influenced by many different religions, as was
Christianity, but Jewish eschatological beliefs can be defini-
tively traced to Zoroastrianism. Founded sometime in the
seventh century B.C.E., this religion represents the oldest apocalyptic tradition that we will deal with here. Zoroastrianism survived in
Persia (modern Iran) until it was marginalized by Islam during the
seventh century C.E., yet remnants of adherents still remain.

Zoroastrian eschatology is the oldest eschatology in recorded history, originating around 500 B.C.E. The religion itself
was founded on the teachings of the prophet, Zoroaster, or Zara-
thustra, and this religion is also known as *Mazdaism*. Its god was
known as *Ahura Mazda*. Zoroaster claimed that God was all good,
in Whom no evil could dwell. Judaism gradually adopted this theology, which was then passed down to Christianity and Islam.

The theology of radical dualism (that there are two forces in
the Universe, one good and one evil) which became the basis of
all three Abrahamic religions, was a purely Zoroastrian invention.
Even the personification of evil as an opposing force to God was
invented by Zoroaster. The Persian *Angra Mainyu* was the precur-

sor of the Jewish Satan.

Ahura Mazda, like *Yahweh* and *Allah* patterned after him, is a distant god—never immanent in the world. He was all good and he created a perfect world which only later became corrupted by evil. Evil will eventually resolve back into the good, and into oneness with *Ahura Mazda*—a concept that has more in common with Gnosticism than with Judaism, Christianity and Islam.

Zoroastrianism eschatology also differs from that of the Abrahamic faiths in not allowing for divine intervention. Human beings had to save themselves. That the individual is responsible for the fate of his own soul, also means that he simultaneously shares in the responsibility for the fate of the world.

Not a great deal is known about Zoroastrian eschatology, and what is known comes from a surviving fragment of a text known as the *Bundhahishn*. In this religious system there are three ages: creation, mixture and separation. There will be a final battle between the forces of good (the *yazatas*) and the forces of evil (the *daevas*) and the good will triumph.

There will be a general resurrection of the dead, after which both the living and the dead will face final judgment. The mountains will become molten metal rivers. The righteous will cross the river of fire without harm, while those who had done evil in life would fall into it and burn.

The molten river will continue to flow all the way down to hell itself. There it will annihilate all of the evil that is still left in the world. The righteous remnant will become immortal, will hunger or thirst no more, and become so light they will not even cast a shadow. All those who have been saved will speak one language in a world without borders. They will have a common purpose, and that is the exaltation of God. While there is a restoration of original creation, there will be no absorption into the Godhead. Everything that was brought into existence by *Ahura Mazda* will continue to have a separate existence.

According to redactions in the text known as the *Zand-i Vohuman:*

> At the end of the tenth hundredth winter . . . the sun is
> more unseen and more spotted; the years, months, and
> days are shorter, and the earth is more barren. Crops will
> not yield seeds, and men . . . become more deceitful and
> more given to violent practices. They have no gratitude.
> Honorable wealth will all proceed to those of perverted
> faith . . . and a dark cloud makes the whole sky night . . .
> and it will rain more noxious creatures than winter.

While the Abrahamic faiths adopted the idea of a final battle between the forces of good and the forces of evil, Zoroastrian eschatology was not nearly as vindictive as Judaism, Christianity and Islam. Sinners were to be punished for only three days, *after which they would be forgiven!*

In Zoroastrianism, a further universal judgment would take place, and it would decide the fate of the whole world. After this judgment, a new world of perfection would appear, in which poverty, old age, disease, thirst, hunger and death would be banished.

Zoroastrians believed that the total history of the world would be summed up in twelve thousand years, which were divided into four distinct periods of three thousand years each. During the first period only goodness prevails. During the second period, evil comes into the world. The third period is a period when good and evil people will war against each other. The beginning of the fourth period was marked by the birth of Zoroaster, and this period is not yet finished. During the final three thousand year period, three saviors will appear, one for each millennium.

The last savior to appear will be *Soshyant*, who will defeat the forces of evil and resurrect the dead. At the end, molten metal will purify the earth and return it to a perfect and unified state.

The gift of immortality will be conferred when *Soshyant*, acting as a priest, celebrates the final sacrifice with the last animal (an ox) to die in the service of man. The Savior will mix the fat of the ox with white *Haoama* (a sacred mixture used in ceremonies) to create the elixir of immortality.

After the earth has been leveled by the molten metal, the demons *Ahriman* and *Azhi* will run to Hell to escape the flow, only to be overcome by it. After the earth is leveled and humans restored to their ideal unity of body and soul, the whole creation will again be the perfect combination of spirit and matter that God intended it to be.

Chapters

Store# 00935 Chapters Sudbury
1425 Kingsway Road
Sudbury,ON P3A 4R7
Phone: (705) 525-5616

You could win $1000 or an iPod!
Complete our survey at
www.indigofeedback.com
or call 1-877-402-1486.
See site for contest rules.

Store# 00935 Term# 002 Trans# 131856
Operator: 206JM   08/14/2012 13:53
PLUM REWARDS SALE
5000****5215

****

END OF DAYS $15.40G
9780984375431

****

Items: 1

Subtotal:		$15.40
GST:	5.0%	$0.77
Total:		**$16.17**
CASH:		**$20.00**
Change:		$3.83

****

Member No.: 5000****5215

plum points earned:	154
Total plum points earned today:	**154**
Current plum points balance:	5798
Next reward level:	8500

****

Like Us On Facebook!

Store# 00935 Term# 002 Trans# 131856
GST Registration # R897152666

009350020131856 1

Points Required	Reward Value
2,500	$5
4,500	$10
8,500	$20
20,000	$50
35,000	$100

Explore the benefits of plum rewards and become a member for free! Visit indigo.ca/plumrewards to learn more.

Chapters !ndigo COLES indigo.ca

Refunds or exchanges may be made within 14 days if item is returned in store-bought condition with a receipt. Items with a gift receipt may be exchanged or refunded onto a credit note for the value of the item at the time of purchase. We cannot provide an exchange or refund on magazines or newspapers.

plum™ rewards

Points Required	Reward Value
2,500	$5
4,500	$10
8,500	$20
20,000	$50
35,000	$100

Explore the benefits of plum rewards and become a member for free! Visit indigo.ca/plumrewards to learn more.

Chapters !ndigo COLES indigo.ca

VI. Radical Dualism and the Invention of Satan

But who prays for Satan? Who, in eighteen centuries
has had the common humanity to pray for the
one sinner that needed it most?

- MARK TWAIN

ost people who read the Bible, and especially those who believe in its divine authorship and inerrancy, do not realize that the God of the *Old Testament*, the Hebrew *Bible*, was conceived as being the source of both good and evil. A God that was by definition both omnipotent and omniscient, could never allow any cosmic force to oppose him. The existence of evil, then, could only be explained by assuming that God was both Light and Shadow. His dual nature contains both yin and yang. The biblical God has a dark side, and this is why one should fear him. The prophet, Isaiah, made this clear:

> I am YHWH, unrivalled. I form the light and create the
> dark. I make good fortune and I create calamity.
> It is I, YHWH who does all of this.

> *- ISAIAH 45:7*

The theology of radical dualism—the idea that God cannot contain any evil within Himself—is not a biblical idea, nor did it originate in Judaism. It is Zoroastrian in origin. In the year 597 B.C.E., Babylonia conquered the southern Israelite kingdom of Judah and exiled its occupants to their own homeland. In 539 B.C.E., Persia conquered Babylonia and allowed the captive Jews to return home, but not before radically altering their world-view.

Upon returning to their own land, the two southern tribes found themselves in theological conflict with the northern tribes of Israel—who had, themselves, been conquered by Assyria. The results of this new belief system were catastrophic. To deny that God has the power to both create and to destroy made it necessary to create an anti-God, and that was heresy.

This Zoroastrian heresy gradually prevailed over time, but not until after the biblical period had ended. The concept of an opposing force to God does not show up in Jewish literature until the second century B.C.E. By the time of Jesus, the new theology was firmly established in Judaism and the heresy passed into Christianity and, later, Islam.

The Jews who had returned from Babylonia saw clearly that the God of the Bible had an image problem. He was forever going around exterminating people—something quite unbecoming a god. Yahweh needed an extreme makeover, but where could one find a villain to play the fall guy for Him? The new theologians scoured the scriptures and finally made their selection. The newly minted cosmic bad guy was the completely innocent angel, Satan!

For the makeover of Yahweh to work, Satan had to receive the same treatment, but in reverse. Satan, as a popular image of an evil cosmic force, has survived the ages right down to the present time, and yet this image of Satan is not biblical.

The transformation of Satan serves as a good example of biblical texts which were often manipulated to serve the theological needs of the day. Satan in the Hebrew *Bible* was neither a fallen angel nor God's adversary. And Satan as the "Prince of Darkness" is entirely a Christian invention.

In the history of Judaism, Satan was first introduced in the *Book of Job*, a work written between 1000-800 B.C.E. In *Job*, Satan is God's undercover agent—his "accuser," or prosecuting attorney. Nowhere in the *Old Testament* is Satan God's adversary. He was always a member in good standing among God's holy entourage.

In the biblical *Book of Job*, God sends Satan to test Job's faith, although it is only fair to point out that Satan did have God's ear, and more or less talked Him into letting Satan do the dirty work. Still, it was God who gave the orders, and Satan merely carried them out.

In the story, Job was known as a man of great faith. He gave credit for everything that had gone right in his life, not to himself, but to God. But Satan, thinking out loud in the presence of God, wondered if Job would still have such great faith in Him if the rug were pulled out from under his feet. What would happen, Satan asked God, if Job no longer had all the good things in life: health, prosperity, and a loving family? What would happen if God took all these things away? Would Job still praise God, or would he curse Him instead?

God muses over this question for awhile and finally gives

Satan permission to go down and make Job's life a living hell. So Job becomes sick, he loses all his wealth, and God kills a number of his family members. As expected, Job became a pathetic wretch, and when his fiends visit they ask him what great sins he had committed that God should punish him so. Job tells them that he has done nothing wrong at all. In that case, Job's friends advise, he should curse God. But Job refuses.

In the end, Satan is proven wrong. Job never blames God for his misery and he never loses his faith. Seeing Job's great faith in the face of such adversity, God is greatly impressed and gives back everything he had taken from him except, of course, those family members who are now deceased. The biblical God never thinks about raising anyone from the dead. In the Hebrew *Bible*, dead is dead.

The story of Job is really about a human being outmaneuvering not only one of God's major angels, but God Himself. Job excelled as a righteous man and attained a higher state of spiritual being by surviving all of his travails with an appreciable amount of grace still intact. And that is the point of the story: don't blame God, don't blame yourself—just accept what life throws at you.

Satan appears again in the Biblical book of *Numbers* (550-400 B.C.E.) in *Zechariah* (6th century B.C.E.) and in *I Chronicles* (400-250 B.C.E.) In no instance is Satan any more than God's "accuser." He never becomes a fallen angel, and he certainly doesn't become God's adversary. In one case, in fact, Satan even protects a person against evil. (*Numbers* 22:23-33)

The Jews were still more or less stuck with a sociopathic deity because they couldn't exactly rewrite the entire *Bible*. They could, however, change a thing here and there, and maintain denial of everything else. One instance of biblical manipulation is *I Chronicles* 21:1. Here, some scribe replaced the original words of the text, "the anger of the Lord," with the word, "Satan." We know that this happened because the original story, with its original wording, can be found in the *earlier* work of 2 *Samuel* 24:1.

To really launch Satan's new career, however, Christians were needed. In the *New Testament*, and in the early Church, Satan was made the scapegoat for everything and everyone Christians despised. They even created revisionist history by claiming that the Serpent in the Garden of Eden was really Satan in disguise.

Even though there are no references in the *Bible*, the author of Luke's Gospel, writing around 90 C.E., boldly claimed that Satan was a fallen angel: "I beheld Satan fall as lightning from heaven" (*Luke* 10:18). The author of *Luke* did not invent this idea—earlier Jews did—but *Luke* made the idea popular.

The early Church fathers used Satan to strike out at every imaginable Christian group or teacher they considered heretical. The self-appointed apostle of Christ, Paul, began such attacks as early as 50 C.E. In his second letter to the *Corinthians* (11:13-15), Paul accused all Christians who didn't agree with him of being agents of Satan:

> [They are] false apostles, deceptive workers, disguising themselves as apostles of Christ. And no wonder! Even Satan himself disguises himself as an angel of light. So it is not strange if his servants disguise themselves as servants of righteousness.

Writing around 180 C.E., the Church father, Irenaeus, Bishop of Lyons, in his famous and extensive treatise, *Adversus Haereses, (Against Heresy)* attacked Gnostic Christian theology as something that "infects hearers with bitter and malignant poison of the serpent, inspired by Satan." Christians have used Satan to attack heretics ever since.

In addition to Satan, later Jewish authors borrowed, and pressed into service, all manner of mythical monsters that belonged to various religions with which they had come into

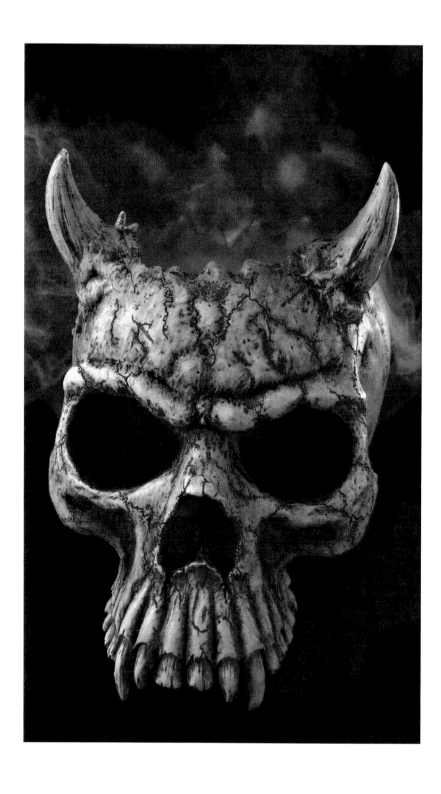

contact. The dragon that plays a lead role in John's *Revelation* was invented by the Persians. The Leviathan, also in *Revelation*, was the chaos monster of the Egyptians. Still other monsters were borrowed from Canaanite mythology.

When Alexander the Great conquered the land of Israel, he found two opposing factions of Jews. One faction—those of the northern kingdom of Israel who had never been exiled to Babylonia—wanted to assimilate with other ethnic peoples and cultures. The southern tribes of Judah which returned from Babylonia with their heresy of radical dualism were strictly against any and all assimilation, and that attitude has prevailed in Judaism.

Satan promoters based their strange theology on a passage in *Genesis* (6:2) where angels come down from heaven, see that human women are beautiful, and *mate* with them! According to the story, this bizarre sexual coupling produced a race of giants who, because of their act, lost their angelic powers. Jews after 167 B.C.E. began to argue that these god/men were monsters and, as monsters, must be a legion of evil. Along with Satan, these fallen angels became convenient scapegoats and got the blame for all human violence, greed and lust.

Gnostic Christians took a different tact altogether. They proposed that Yahweh was just evil, period—without any redeeming features at all. The creator God of the Bible was himself the anti-god, always full of malice. They argued that Yahweh created human bodies for the sole purpose of trapping human souls (which are sparks of divine Light) in a prison of flesh, and further causing them to forget their true nature as part of the All.

The Gnostic, Basilides, tried to undo the Jewish heresy by teaching that all things, all dualities, were naturally existing complements and, in one way or another, all things existed within God whom he called *Abraxas*. *Abraxas* contained all potential and all action, all existence and all non-existence.

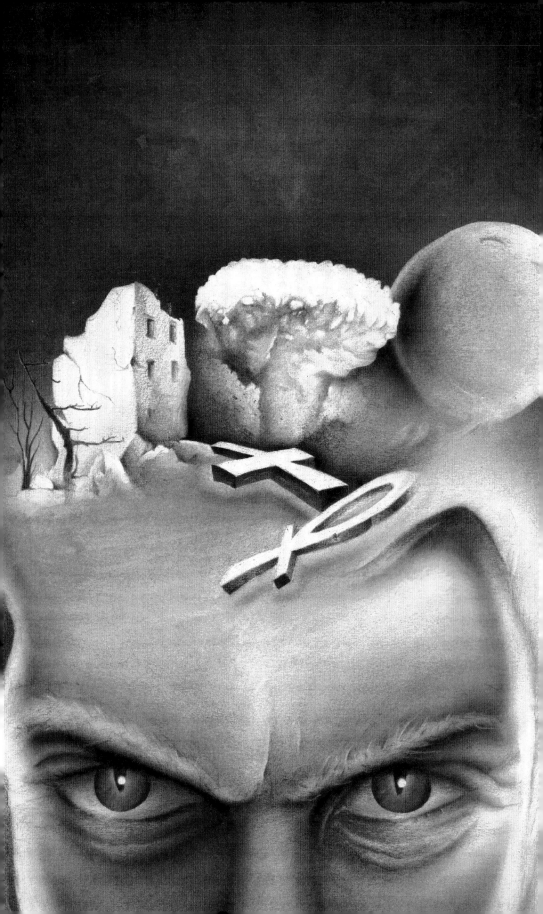

VII. The Nature of Evil

Nature, in her indifference, makes no distinction between good and evil.

- ANATOLE FRANCE

Basilides' theology was much closer to the philosophy of Hinduism and Buddhism which has always taught there is but a single Reality in the Universe. All matter and energy emanate from this same Source. That being the case, both Hinduism and Buddhism deny that evil has any ultimate reality. It may seem to exist in the phenomenal world, but only to the human mind. As Shakespeare put it, "There is no good nor bad, but thinking makes it so."

In Eastern philosophy, human suffering is not the result of evil either. Suffering is the result of our attachment to things that are subject to change, decay and dissolution. Everything in the material realm is impermanent in nature, but humans do not generally understand this. They suffer because they become attached to things that cannot last.

Taoism emphasizes that we suffer because of our resistance to the ever-flowing river of change, which is *Tao—That Which Is*. Resisting change is the cause of all human frustration and suffering. "Evil," then, is nothing more, nor less, than a symptom of disharmony—whether it is within the human body, or within the greater human body of society. If we were able to embrace each and every change that came to us in life, then we would be living in harmony of *Tao—The Way Things Are*. If we did not discriminate between what we like and what we dislike, our suffering would cease. We would view one state of affairs as no better or worse than another.

Dualistic consciousness causes disharmony within the whole, and it is this thinking that is destroying the world we live in. Humans evolved (or devolved) as the result of changes to the environment, natural disasters, the invention of language, war, migration, the creation of agrarian societies and any number of new challenges that forced us to leave our sense of oneness behind and embrace separateness. When we began to see ourselves as separate from all life we became neurotic, and even insane.

> If you wish to see the truth, then hold no opinions for, or against, anything. To set up what you like against what you dislike is the disease of the mind. When the deep meaning of things is not understood, the mind's essential peace is disturbed to no avail.

> - THE THIRD CHINESE PATRIARCH OF ZEN

In the *Gospel of Thomas*, Jesus tells his disciples:

> This heaven will pass away and that which is above it will pass away. The dead are not alive, and the living will not die. In the days when you ate what is dead, you made it alive. When you come into the light, what will you do? On the day when you were one, you became two. But when you have become two what will you do?

At another point, he proposes a solution:

When you make the two one, and when you make the inner like the outer and the outer like the inner, and the upper like the lower, and when you make the male and the female into a single one . . . then will you enter the kingdom.

Harkening back to the days of innocence when we didn't believe that nakedness was shameful, Jesus says:

When you undress without being ashamed, and take your clothes and put them under your feet the way little children do and trample on them, then you will see the son of the living one and you will not be afraid.

VIII. In the Beginning Was the End: The Apocalypse in Light of the Genesis Creation Myths

The disciples said to Jesus, "Tell us how our end will come. "Jesus said, "Have you discovered the beginning, that you should search for the end? In the place where the beginning is, there the end will be. Blessed is he who will stand at the beginning. He will know the end and will not taste death."

- THE GOSPEL OF THOMAS

For Christians, apocalyptic expectation is directly related to the Christian doctrine of "original sin." A new world is necessary because this one has been corrupted by none other than first members of our species. Our sinful nature is genetic, irreparable, and fatal. All we can do is cast ourselves upon the grace and mercy of God—so that He will create a new world in which sin does not exist.

The Christian doctrine of original sin is based on the belief that the creation story—the second one, not the first—should be taken at face value, rather than being understood as the allegory it is. Anyone willing to read the *Genesis* myth without Christian prejudice will realize that the story about Adam and Eve is not only profound, but has nothing to do with humanity's rebellion against God.

First, however, we need to consider the *first* creation story in

Genesis which begins at 1:1 and ends at 2:3. This is the more recent of the two creation myths, probably written around 500 B.C.E., and coming from the Priestly stream of early Jewish tradition. The second creation myth—the story of Adam and Eve—was written some four hundred years earlier. Certainly the Jewish theologians who organized and finalized the biblical canon knew when these stories were written, so we can only wonder as to their chronology.

It seems significant, however, that the very first story in the Bible has a number of unique features. First of all, the Creator in this story is not Yahweh, but *Elohim*—literally, "the gods." Unlike the second creation narrative, the Creator in this story places no restrictions upon what the man and woman on earth can and cannot do, or what they can or cannot eat—although vegetarianism is highly recommended. (Gen. 1:29)

Since there are no rules, no good and no evil, the first couple do not sin and do not fall from the Creator's grace. Quite the opposite is the case: the gods are very pleased with every aspect of their creation, especially their greatest work: Homo sapiens.

Unlike in the second myth, the first woman in this narrative is created at the same time as the first man—not later, as a divine afterthought. Neither is this version of the first woman created *from* man (Adam's rib in the second narrative), so this story provides no basis for ancient man's insistence on woman's subservience. Neither are the first couple created from the "dust of the Earth," as they are in the second myth, but from divine substance.

As a name for God, *Elohim* appears many more times in the Hebrew Bible than does YHWH (*Yahweh*). In most instances *Elohim* refers to a single God, but that is not the case in the two *Genesis* creation myths. Linguistic scholars have shown conclusively that in these instances *Elohim* (and in the second story, the creator is called *Iahveh*, and represents twenty names which make up the council of gods acting in concert) is a plurality and refers to a pantheon of gods, or a "plurality" of gods, or a Mother/Father

Godhead. The last seems more likely since "male and female were created by the gods in their image" which means the "image" of God is made of both masculine and feminine forces.

> Then Elohim (the gods) said, "Let us create man in our image, after our likeness." (*Genesis* 1:26)

> So God [Elohim] created man in his [their] own image, in the image of God [the gods] created him; male and female he created them." (*Genesis* 1:27)

That humanity was created in the image of the gods means that humanity was created out of "divine substance." At the very least, humanity was created as a *reflection* of divinity. The divinity which is reflected is androgynous, being both masculine and feminine.

With this understanding, it is not hard to see why orthodox Christianity ignored, and continues to ignore, the first chapter of the *Bible*. This story provides no basis for the theology of original sin. Neither does it support the Church's patriarchal hierarchy. Moreover, this creation myth is altogether heretical: the Creator is an androgynous Godhead, and human beings are created as gods.

As we all know, the second creation myth—which begins at Genesis 2:4—is an altogether different story. But has it been interpreted correctly by Christianity? I do not believe so. Instead of being a story about humanity's rebellion against God, it is actually an allegory that accurately mythologizes humanity's evolutionary history!

Christians take it at face value that Adam (Hebrew: *Adham*, which means "humanity") and Eve (Mother of all) willfully disobeyed God by eating fruit from the one tree in the whole Garden of Eden which God tells them they must not eat. But this would have been impossible since Adam and Eve wouldn't have known the difference between obeying and disobeying.

The first couple could not commit an evil act by eating from the Tree of the Knowledge of Good and Evil because they didn't know there was any difference between good and evil. For Adam and Eve, there was no malice aforethought, no wrong intention, no premeditation, no intent to disobey and, therefore, no sin. Would the author have been so careless and ignorant as to not notice the inconsistencies of his own story? Or did he intend his audience to understand the story in a different way altogether?

The illogic continues with the Creator's warning that if Adam and Eve ate the fruit of this one tree they would die; that is—become subject to death. Such a warning would have been meaningless because Adam and Eve had no experience of death.

The author of this creation myth implies that the gods were not very godlike. If they were real gods, they would have had foreknowledge of Adam and Eve's blunder, so they would never have created the forbidden tree in the first place. If they had known the Serpent would tempt Adam and Eve, they would not have created the Serpent. There is only one reason for these literary blunders: the story is *designed* to function as a set-up for Adam and Eve's faux pax. The first couple were purposely framed! Adam and Eve were entirely innocent of wrong doing. The evildoers, if any at all, are the gods themselves, as they often are in ancient mythology. They set a trap knowing that their recent creations would fall right into it.

If the allegory isn't about original sin, disobedience or a fall from grace, what was the story's purpose? For the theologically unbiased reader, the symbolism virtually jumps off the page. The Garden of Eden represents primeval nature. Adam and Eve represent the innocence of humanity during that period of our evolution when our consciousness was still aboriginal. In the beginning we saw ourselves as being one with all things. We did not make distinctions between good and evil or between spirit and matter. We were hunter-gatherers, living off the land in complete harmony with nature.

Eating from the "Tree of the Knowledge of Good and Evil" is a metaphor for the moment in human evolution when Homo sapiens began to view the world dualistically. When we separated from our aboriginal state, it was evolution that banished us from Paradise.

Since many of the elements of the Genesis creation myth are founded on the Babylonian creation story, *Enuma Elish*, the metaphor of the Serpent who tempted Eve to eat the forbidden fruit probably came from this source as well. In the Babylonian myth, the Serpent, *Ningishzida*, is a friend to *Adapa* (Adam=Mankind), and helps him search for immortality. The brazen serpent, Nehushtan, stood at the Temple in Jerusalem, and was the object of worship until the time of Hezekiah.

The Serpent that "tempted" Eve, then, may be seen as an angelic creature. In the book of *Enoch*, the angelic Seraphim are winged serpents. The gods in the *Genesis* myth punish the Serpent by making it crawl on the ground, suggesting that it did not do so previously.

It is even more likely that the Serpent belonged to the highest order of angelic being—the Seraphim—in that they are related to the Cherubim, lesser angels the gods placed in the Garden to guard the Tree of Life. Cherubim always appear in conjunction with Seraphim in biblical literature, and since Seraphim are not specifically mentioned in this myth, it is likely the Serpent was, in fact, a representative of the Seraphim.

While Seraphim were flying serpents with six pairs of wings, Cherubim, in the book of *Ezekiel*, are winged creatures with a tetrad of faces: lion, ox, eagle and man. They have four wings, hands like humans, and the feet of calves. In other literature, the Cherubim are winged creatures with the head of a bull, the wings of an eagle, the feet of a lion, and the tail of a serpent. With biblical mythology, nothing is what it seems.

The Tree of Life, with roots that reach to the center of the earth, and branches that reach the heavens, represents humanity's quest for immortality, which is ultimately denied by the jealous creator-gods. The set-up begins with the gods creating Eve as a way of splitting Adam (humankind) in two, thereby destroying humanity's original androgynous consciousness. In order to create woman (womb-man), the gods cause Adam to fall into a "deep sleep," which may be interpreted as ignorance of his original nature. So the separation of woman from man in this story represents the loss of our original unitary consciousness.

> Jesus said, "On the day when you were one, you became two. But when you have become two, what will you do?"
>
> *- THE GOSPEL OF THOMAS*

After Adam and Eve are banished from the Garden—after humanity became separate from the natural order—they gave birth to two sons: Cain and Able. Cain is forced to till the soil, and represents the end of our hunter-gatherer period as a species and the beginning of agrarian societies. Able is a sheepherder and represents pastoral societies. Cain killing Able is a metaphor for the dominance of agrarian societies over pastoral societies.

Cain is now cursed, and becomes the curse ("the mark of Cain"). With the growth of human populations over the centuries there was an endless need for more land on which to raise crops. The only way to acquire more land was to steal it from its rightful owners. To feed the masses, war became a necessity. As Jared Diamond points out in his book, *Guns, Germs and Steel*, the creation of agrarian societies was the single most devastating development in human history. The need to dominate and manipulate nature eventually led to industrialization. Industrialization led to technology, and technology is leading us directly into the apocalypse.

According to Ben Kieman in his book, *Blood and Soil: A World History of Genocide and Extermination from Sparta to Darfur*, ancient societies' preoccupation with land use pitted prospective farmers against ethnically alien town dwellers. This was the case when Israel conquered the land of Canaan. The Canaanites were a pastoral society at the time they were overrun by the warlike Hebrews.

The theology of original sin is not biblical; it is not Jewish and it was not even believed by all early Christians. The concept of original sin is a great injustice, entirely invented by the early Church. This is not to say that human beings have a dark side. They certainly do, and so they must suppress their shadow in order to defeat the cherubim and the flaming sword, and seize the Tree of Life. Gods or no gods, our destiny is in our own hands. Surely the author of this creation myth knew that.

Carl Jung once wrote,

> The only thing that really matters now is whether man can climb up to a higher moral level, to a higher plane of consciousness, in order to be equal to the superhuman powers which the fallen angels have placed into his hands. But he can make no progress until he becomes very much better acquainted with his own nature.

For Jung, the apocalypse is a psychic event. The ultimate battle between good and evil must take place within ourselves. The roads to Armageddon and Paradise are both laid out before us. We are now at the fork the road. Which path will our species ultimately take?

Jesus said,

> If you bring forth what is within you, what you bring forth will save you. If you do not bring forth what is within you, what you do not bring forth will destroy you.

> *- THE GOSPEL OF THOMAS*

IX. An Introduction to Judeo/Christian Apocalyptic Literature

Each religion, by the help of more or less myth,
which it takes more or less seriously, proposes some
method of fortifying the human soul and enabling
it to make is peace with its destiny.

- GEORGE SANTAYANA

The Greek word, "apocalypse" means "revelation," and that is the actual title of the last book of *The New Testament* that is variously, but wrongly, referred to as *The Book of Revelations*, *Revelations* or *The Revelation of John.* It was not written by "Saint" John, Jesus' disciple, but by an anonymous John, writing from the island of Patmos near the end of the first century C.E. John's *Apocalypse* was neither the first nor the last work of its kind. Apocalyptic literature as genre had a four hundred year history— originating during the second century B.C.E., and ending during the second century C.E.

The Book of Daniel in the Hebrew *Bible* is the earliest example of a true Jewish apocalypse, and the author of *Revelation* borrowed many of Daniel's images and symbols. Other Jewish apocalypses include sections of the Biblical books of *Ezekiel* and *Zechariah*, and the apocryphal *Books of Enoch, The Apocalypse of Weeks, The Apocalypse of Noah, The Assumption of Moses, The Apocalypse of Ezra* (2 *Ezdra* 3:14) and *The Apocalypse of Baruch.* Many of these texts were discovered at Qumran in 1947, as were part of the so-called Dead Sea Scrolls. The Qumran community also produced its own apocalypse known as *The War Scroll*.

Neither was John's *Revelation* the only Christian apocalypse. Christians also produced *The Ascension of Isaiah*, *The Apocalypse of Peter*, the *First* and *Sixth Books of Esra*, the *Christian Sibyllines*, *The Book of Elchasai*, *The Coptic Gnostic Apocalypse of Paul*, *The Coptic Gnostic Apocalypse of Peter*, *The Apocalypse of Paul* and the *Apocalypse of Thomas*.

Sixty-five percent of all apocalyptic imagery found in *Revelation* was not original to the author, but was taken directly from

the Old Testament, that is, the Hebrew *Bible*. In *Ezekiel* we find the apocalyptic imagery of the "four living creatures" (man, lion, ox, eagle), as well as the John's "scrolls," the "great harlot," and "blasphemous kingdoms."

John's image of hordes of destructive locusts was taken from the biblical *Book of Joel*, and the images of lamp-stands, scrolls, and four horses of different colors came from *The Book of Zechariah.*

The extra-canonical book of *I Enoch*, written during the third century B.C.E., is the earliest example of the Jewish beliefs about a final judgment of the wicked and fallen angels:

> Behold, he comes with ten thousands of his saints, to execute judgment upon them, and destroy the wicked, and reprove everything which the sinful and ungodly have done, and committed against him.

- I ENOCH 3:1

The Book of Daniel, written around 165 B.C.E., and the author of *Revelation* borrowed Daniel's monstrous beasts, the crowning of the "son of man," and the vision of seventy weeks of years. Even the concept of the Jewish Messiah, and his "second coming" were suggested by the author of *Daniel*:

> I saw in night visions, and behold, in the clouds of heaven there came one like a son of man, and he came to the Ancient of Days and was presented before him. And to him was given dominion and glory and king-dom, that all peoples, nations and languages should serve him; his dominion is an everlasting dominion which shall not pass away, and his kingdom is one that shall not be destroyed.

DANIEL 7:13-14

The Qumran community, in its *War Scroll* introduced the idea of a final cosmic war between "sons of light" and the "sons of darkness." Subsequent Jewish apocalypses like *IV Ezra* and *II Baruch* were written after the destruction of Jerusalem in 70 C.E., quite close to the time when John wrote his famous *Revelation* (85-95 C.E.). The image of the "Beast" as a reference to Rome was common to all three apocalypses.

All apocalypses—both Jewish and Christian—were written as responses to foreign occupation, oppression and persecution. The author of *Daniel* wrote during a period when Israel was occupied by the Greek forces of Macedonia under the leadership of Antiochus in 167 B.C.E. When Jesus was crucified by the Romans as a messianic pretender in 30 C.E., the Holy Land was occupied by Rome, and all Christian apocalypses were responses to Roman persecution.

Every apocalypse claims to have been written by a seer or prophet whose "revelation" comes to him during a vision, dream or an out-of-body experience. The stories usually include a mediator, such as an angel, who speaks directly to the visionary.

The individual revelations were not meant to be self-explanatory but were written in coded language which consisted of arcane symbols, fantastic creatures and esoteric numbers. These images, symbols and numbers cannot be understood apart from the biblical references from which they came.

Apocalypses were not written as predictions of future events, but as reactions to present circumstances. John's *Revelation*, for instance, was written to seven specific churches in Asia Minor, not to other churches in other parts of the Empire. His mythological symbols and coded language were reader specific.

John's audience understood the full meaning of his symbolism because they were well versed in earlier Jewish apocalyptic literature, as well as the Hebrew *Bible*. His text was directly related to political events and social movements well known by the congregants of the seven churches, and has no meaning outside of this context.

Literary texts are meant to address the expectation of their audience. One does not read a newspaper in the same way one reads a poem. Because of the genre he is working in, the apocalyptic author of *Revelation* uses and reuses the symbols and styles of earlier apocalyptic authors. The misinterpretation of *Revelation* in modern times is due to reading "the apocalypse" as if it were a book of magic or secret lore—which it is not. Like any other apocalypse, there are no secret codes to be decoded in *Revelation* that would be relevant to us today. John was not predicting that the world would end sometime in the future; it was ending now! There would be *no* future.

X. The End of Days in Judaism

In six thousand years, all things will be finished.

- PSEUDO-BARNABAS

T he War Scroll, part of the *Dead Sea Scrolls*, can tell us how and why Jews of that period—and during the time of Jesus—looked forward to the apocalypse. The War Scroll, and the scroll that followed it, *The Rule of War*, not only predicted the end of days, but included a complete manual of arms and order of battle for the final war against all of Israel's enemies. Those separatists who lived at the Wadi Qumran understood their reality as an antithesis between the forces of light and the forces of darkness.

The War Scroll is primarily about the coming "Day of Vengeance." The Jews at Qumran understood that to mean the extermination of all oppressors, especially Rome. On the great Day of Vengeance, "the priests shall continue to blow the trumpets of massacre."

To reverse their humiliation by one foreign occupier after another, the Jews of Qumran relished in their dreams of vengeance. When the Day of Vengeance came, the kings of other nations would "lick the dust of your feet." The Jewish God would "burn the sinners in the perdition of hell, in an eternal blaze . . . in all the eternal seasons."

On the *Day of Revenge*, "Israel has called out the sword against all the nations" . . . "Lay Thine hand on the neck of Thine enemies and Thy feet on the pile of the slain! Smite the nations, Thine adversaries, and devour flesh with Thy sword!"

In Judaism, the end of the world is called the *acharit hayamim*, the "end of days." In these days, all manner of tumultuous events will occur to overturn the current world order and make way for a new world in which *Yahweh* will be universally recognized as the ruler over everyone and everything.

The *Avodah Zarah* of the *Talmud* states that from start to finish, the world will exist only six thousand years. By the Jew's calendar, 5772 years have already passed, so the apocalypse should take place in the year 2240 C.E.

Before the end, all Jewish in exile will return to Israel, after which Israel will war against and defeat all of her enemies. Jews will then build a third Temple and resume their ancient practice of making sacrificial offerings. The dead will be raised on the Day of Resurrection, and the Jewish Messiah will become King of Israel. Israel will then be attacked by the mythical kingdom of *Gog*, led by its king, *Magog*. This battle will be the beginning of the great cosmic war of *Armageddon* (a mythical location.)

Israel will win this war, and once *Yahweh* defeats His enemies, He will end the existence of all who do evil in the world. At the end of the 6,000 year period, a seventh millennium will begin—a new era of holiness, tranquility, spiritual life and worldwide peace called the *Olam Haba*, or "Future World." In this new age all people will come to know God directly.

...beloved, remember ye the
...mockers in the last time...
...walk after their own
...they who separate...
that they told you there...

...keep you from falling...
...you faultless before the...
...his glory with exceeding...
24 Now unto him...
25 To the only wise God
Saviour, be glory and
dominion and power, both
now and ever. Amen.

THE REVELATION OF
JOHN THE DIVINE

...Jesus Christ,
...unto him,
...things
...to pass...
...by his...

7 Behold, he cometh with clouds;
and every eye shall see him, and
they also which pierced him: and
all kindreds of the earth shall...
I am Alpha and Omega...

XI. Understanding the Book of *Revelation*

The Bible *is a wonderful source of inspiration for those who don't understand it.*

- GEORGE SANTAYANA

A s previously mentioned, apocalypses cannot be understood outside of their historical context. John's *Revelation* was written to seven specific churches in Asia Minor, sometime between 70 C.E. and 100 C.E. The intent of John's letter, in the form of an apocalypse, was to address the specific concerns of these churches and encourage their faith during a time of adversity. John also used this occasion to attack his enemies—one being the Nicolatians, a Gnostic Christian sect that John apparently "hated."

John was informing his seven Christian congregations that the end times had already begun, and much of his mythological allusions are based on events that had *already* taken place. The end of the present world would not take place in the distant future, it would take place during the next few days, weeks and months.

John's esoteric message, embedded in apocalyptic imagery, would have been understood by members of the seven churches to which he writes. But if his letter were to fall into the hands of the enemy—the forces of Rome—it would appear to be nothing more than occult prattle.

Romans would not understand the real meaning of John's *Revelation* any more than present day Christians do. Like all apocalyptic authors, John's coded message would only make sense to those who knew the key to the code—those believers already steeped in the apocalyptic imagery of such sacred texts as *Ezekiel*, *Zechariah, Daniel, Ezdras* and *Enoch*. Gentiles unfamiliar with such biblical texts could not understand these images in John's *Revelation* and had no interest in trying.

The problem of dating *Revelation* precisely lies in the fact that some of John's references seem to suggest a period shortly after the end of the first Jewish/Roman war (66-70 C.E.) when Nero was emperor of Rome. Other references seem to point to the period of time when Domitian was Emperor. 666, the "number of the Beast," almost certainly refers to Nero since the numbers corresponding to the letters of his name in Hebrew turn out to be 666. As time passed, however, the "Beast" simply stood for Rome in general.

On July 19th in the year 64 C.E., fire broke out in Rome in the squalid cluster of shops around the Circus Maximus. Many accused Nero of starting the fire, but this is unlikely. Fancying himself as a great musician, Nero did, in fact, fiddle while Rome burned. His palace was located on Vatican Hill, and Nero enjoyed the view. But someone had to be blamed for the fires, so Nero picked the small community of Christians who were already widely despised—especially by Jews—in Rome. Some Christians were crucified, others were dressed in animal skins and put into an arena to be torn apart by wild dogs, and still others were covered with pitch and set on fire. These Christians were then placed in Nero's gardens to serve as night lights for the Emperor's parties.

While Christians in Rome were being persecuted during Nero's reign, there were no persecutions taking place in those cities in Asia Minor where John's churches were located—Ephesus, Smyrna, Pergamum, Thyatira, Sardis, Philadelphia and Laodicea.

At many points in his writing, John suggests an Empire-wide persecution of Christians, and that would have been the case when Domitian was Emperor (81-96 C.E.) These anomalies lead some scholars to speculate that John's letter was not composed all at one time, but over a period of several decades.

More support for this later date comes from the writings of the Church father, Irenaeus. Writing in 180 C.E., he claimed that the letter "was seen no long time ago, but almost in our own day, towards the end of Domitian's reign." And Irenaeus, himself, used the same code name for Rome as John did: Babylon.

While the primary purpose of apocalypses was to warn believers of the imminent end of the present world, that was not their only purpose. The apocalyptic message was meant to strengthen the faith in a time of adversity, give spiritual meaning to persecutions and to warn believers of what would happen if they didn't keep their morality intact. And they provided something positive: justice was about to arrive in the world and God would take vengeance against all those who persecuted His people. When all this took place, the world would finally make sense.

John's form of Christianity was probably Jewish, for he still adheres to the Torah and condemns those who do not. John alludes to two different persecutions: one Roman, one Jewish. Beside Roman persecution, Jewish Christians were persecuted by orthodox Jews, considering them to be apostates.

Why were early Christians persecuted in the first place? Romans saw Christians as enemies of the state because they refused to pledge allegiance to the Empire by worshiping—really swearing allegiance to the current emperor as a god. The specific Christians John was addressing also refused to eat food that had been "sacrificed" to idols—according to Jewish law. Such peculiarities helped to set Christians apart from the larger population, and come to the attention of the Roman establishment simply because their behavior, not their beliefs, was seen as being outrageous and traitorous. Christians were even accused of being cannibals, since rumor had it that they ate the body and blood of their god.

Gnostic Christians had none of these problems. They were not persecuted by the Romans, and had no interest in being martyrs. They considered verbal allegiance to the gods of Rome as being a meaningless act and of no real consequence. No temporal power could force them to give up what they believed in their hearts.

What was the ultimate purpose of John's letter? Certainly it was meant to encourage his churches, not only to keep the faith, but to resist the Empire and its pagan rituals. But by chapter twelve of *Revelation*, John's message seems to indicate that everything described in his letter—his entire revelation—had *already* taken place. He proclaims the overthrow of Satan's kingdom and the triumph of God. His "predictions," then, are rhetorical.

Who were John's opponents other than Rome? The "Beast" was code for the Roman Empire in general, but also for the emperor de jour. Besides the hated Nicolatians, mentioned earlier,

"Balaam" is another enemy, but the reference is symbolic: Balaam in Jewish history was accused of encouraging the heresy of mixing ethnic cultures; that is, intermarriage between Jews and all other races. Another enemy is "Jezebel" who had been a pagan queen of Israel and patron of the prophets of *Baal.*

All of these references were really attacks on other Christians whom John considered heretical. "Jezebel," for instance, was John's code word for all Christian female prophets like those Paul railed against in his first letter to the *Corinthians*. John was attacking on multiple fronts: the Roman Empire, Gnostic Christians, feminist Christians and all other Christians with whom he did not agree. One modern feminist author, Tina Pippin, has called *Revelation* a "misogynist fantasy" and believes that "The Apocalypse means death to women."

By the time John finished his letter he had condemned to eternal hellfire every human on Earth who didn't agree with him. His hatred against others led authors like D. H. Lawrence to conclude that *Revelation* was a "repulsive work."

Scholar David L. Barr, in his book, *Revelations: Tales of the End*, states that, "If God triumphs over evil only because God is more powerful than evil, then power—not love or goodness or truth—is the ultimate value of the universe."

There are far too many code words, symbols and images in *Revelation* for us to deal with them all here, but let's at least look at the real meaning of a few of them:

- *Crown:* Not a ruler's crown, but that kind of wreath that was given to victorious athletes.
- *Babylon:* Rome
- *Beast:* Rome and/or individual Roman emperor; especially Nero.
- *Book of Life:* God's record of all that takes place. Also signifies Jewish Christians persecuted by orthodox Jews; as represented

as a curse in an early Jewish liturgy: "May the Nazarenes (followers of Jesus) be blotted out of the Book of Life."

- *Behemoth:* Second ally of the Dragon, who uses deception, seduction and coercion.
- *Dragon:* Chaos monster which the Jews borrowed from Babylonian mythology.
- *Lamp:* Earthly parallel to a heavenly star or angel.
- *Leviathan:* sexual ally of the Dragon.
- *Great Whore:* Jerusalem. The Romans destroyed it, so John is saying that the city and its inhabitants got what they deserved.
- *Lamb:* Jesus
- *Mark of the Beast:* Alludes to the head as the center of the spirit, so those with the mark are those who worship the Beast—the Romans.
- *Morning Star:* Jesus.
- *"Not soiled their clothes":* Christians who had remained pure and chaste.
- *Sealed book:* Common apocalyptic reference. With the seals broken, as they are in John's revelation, the book can now be read, which means the end is near.
- *Seven bowls:* Plagues described in Rev. 16:1-21.
- *Seven heads of the Beast:* The seven hills of Rome.
- *Ten days:* Fullness or completion.
- *Tree of Life:* Both a reference to the creation story in Genesis, and the cross of Jesus.
- *Warriors:* Celibate virgins.
- *6:* The number for incompleteness.
- *666:* The intensification of incompleteness.
- *144,000:* The dimensions of the earthly city of God (twelve times twelve.)

The Apocalypse did not happen in John's time. The Jewish Messiah never arrived. Christ did not return to earth.

In spite of this, there have been Christians and Jews in every age who have never given up hope that the world would end during their own lifetimes. In order to keep this hope alive, predictions of the end have been consistently projected forward in time over the centuries. But even though apocalyptic hope still exists within fundamentalist groups, Christians and Jews generally de-emphasize this part of their religious history. And for good reason: those who endlessly wait for the Apocalypse to arrive are something of an embarrassment to other Jews and Christians. As early as the fourth century, C.E., the Church historian, Eusebius, criticized the second century Christian interpreter, Papias, for harboring such beliefs:

> He says that after the resurrection of the dead there will be a period of a thousand years, when Christ's kingdom will be set up on this earth in material form. I suppose he got these notions by misinterpreting the apostolic accounts and failing to grasp what they had said in mystic and symbolic language. For he seems to have been a man of very small intelligence.

Biblical literalists nevertheless continue to disappoint and embarrass themselves. During the 18th century, the prominent prophet, William Miller (1782-1849), a Baptist lay preacher, predicted that Christ's return to earth would take place in "about 1843." When Christ didn't show, Miller recalculated and set a new date: October 22, 1844. As many as half a million Americans waited for the fateful day and some fifty thousand believers sold or gave away all their earthly possessions, quit their jobs, entered the countryside and waited—all to no avail.

During the 20th century, Hal Lindsey published his very popular and profitable book, *The Late Great Planet Earth*, and predicted the end of the world would take place in 1988. As the date

came nearer and nearer, however, Lindsey equivocated and then finally shut up altogether when nothing happened.

The belief that Jesus is going to return and save us from ourselves has actually contributed to the demise of Earth in present times. As a Christian who read the *Bible* as literal fact and history, James Watt, Ronald Reagan's Secretary of the Interior, stated in private that he had no interest in preserving wilderness because he was certain that Jesus was about to return to Earth. During the past administration there were rumors floating around claiming that George W. Bush had purposely avoided trying to solve the Israeli/Palestinian problem during his tenure because he wanted things to blow up in the Holy Land, believing that the violence would initiate the end times.

The *Left Behind* series of apocalyptic novels written by several different Christian fundamentalists have not only made the authors rich, but have also invented a brand new latter day Christian concept: the "Rapture"—an event where all true Christians (fundamentalists and evangelicals) will ascend into heaven together when the trumpet blows. Their bumper stickers warn drivers in back of them: "In the event of the Rapture, nobody will be behind the wheel."

XII. Later Apocalyptic Movements in Judaism and Christianity

If there is a sin against life, it consists perhaps not so much in despairing of life as in hoping for another life and eluding the implacable grandeur of this life.

- ALBERT CAMUS

During the Middle Ages a new movement known as Brothers of the Free Spirit was branded as heretical because its teachings were considered pantheistic. The Brothers believed that everything was part of God. Since divinity resided in all things, the divinity within living creatures yearned to return to its Divine Source. Like ancient Gnostic Christians, the Brothers longed to return to their divine source and, in doing so, transcend the limits of human existence. Agreeing with Eastern philosophy and Christian Gnosticism, the goal of spiritual work was to return to the Source of our Being.

As a response to the Enlightenment, more new radical Christian movements arose, as did messianic pretenders. During the seventeenth century, and within Puritanism, religious fervor arose in England, and various individuals announced that they were incarnations of God. English apocalyptists declared that God's kingdom was soon to come and would have its center in England.

Oliver Cromwell was one such believer, and this same movement also took root among the Puritans in the New World.

A group called the Diggers was founded during the 1620s by Gerard Winstanley, whose followers wanted to restore mankind to its original state as it had been in the Garden of Eden.

The first Quakers preached a very mystical vision of the future by claiming that God could be approached directly, that an inner divine light existed in each individual, and once it was discovered and nurtured, could achieve salvation on Earth. These believers preached, not about the end of the world, but about a new world order that would take place as people everywhere became enlightened.

Another 17th century group was known as the Ranters, which preached a revolutionary social creed. In 1650, Jacob Bauthumely wrote the treatise, *The Light and Dark Sides of God*. Such movements attacked the idea of God as a cruel authority figure, but dualistic fundamentalism found its voice in a group known as the "Awakening."

To a certain extent, messianic hopes continued in Judaism. In 1666, a Kabbalist from Dulcigno, Montenegro, Shabbetai Zevi, declared himself to be the long awaited Messiah and became leader of a major messianic movement which became popular all across Europe. But Zevi's eccentricities eventually got the better of him, and the rabbis of Smyrna in Asia Minor finally expelled him from their community.

Zevi's messianic aspirations ended abruptly when he was arrested in Gallipoli by the Turks. Zevi, the Jewish Messiah, was given a choice: convert to Islam or die. The Messiah quickly became a Muslim, dashing the hopes of his followers.

The Biblical basis for messianic expectation can be found in *Micah* 4:1-5 (written during the 8th century B.C.E.). Verses 1-3 are also repeated in *Isaiah* 2:2-4. In 3:12, *Micah* predicts the destruction of Jerusalem and then states:

It shall come to pass in the latter days that the mountain of the house of the Lord shall be established as the highest of the mountains and shall be raised up above the hills; and peoples shall flow to it, and many nations shall come, and say: "Come, let us go up to the mountain of the Lord, to the house of the God of Jacob that he may teach us his ways and we may walk in his paths."

For out of Zion shall go forth the law, and the word of the Lord from Jerusalem. He shall judge between many people and shall decide for strong nations afar off; and they shall beat their swords into plowshares, and their spears into pruning hooks; nation shall not lift up sword against nation, neither shall they learn war any more; but they shall sit every man under his vine and under his fig tree and none shall make them afraid; for the mouth of the Lord of hosts has spoken.

For all peoples walk each in the name of its god, but we will walk in the name of the Lord our God for ever and ever.

This passage is significant because of its optimism and universalism. *Micah* saw a future new world of religious tolerance and world peace. Over the next five centuries, however, such hopes for a utopian future on Earth were dashed. In a world without hope, the message became one of cosmic warfare, total destruction, and God's judgment. This is the message that Christians adopted and carried forward to the present day.

XIII. The Final Solution: Islamic Eschatology

I [Mohammed] was commanded to fight people until they say "There is no god but God [Allah], and when they have said it, their lives and their property are protected from me, solely because of it, and judgment upon them is in the hands of God.

- THE KORAN

Behold, God sent me [Mohammed] with a sword just before the Hour [of judgment] and placed my daily sustenance beneath the shadow of my spear, and humiliation and contempt on all those who oppose me.

- THE KORAN

In a very real sense, Islam is the *culmination* of Jewish and Christian apocalypticism and eschatological prediction. Islam was founded on the *apocalyptic* premise: the world cannot be redeemed until it is destroyed. Perpetual jihad—holy war—is necessary to bring about that destruction.

Mohammed spread Islam by the sword and before he died he ordered his followers to conquer the rest of the world within the next one hundred years—for only then, when Islam was the only religion on Earth—would the Day of Judgment come.

As we have already noted, Jewish and Christian eschatology both agree that a new world cannot be ushered in without the destruction of the old world. The current practice of *jihad*, or holy war, promoted and carried out by Islamic "radicals," is not radical. It has been a part of *orthodox* Islamic theology for fourteen hundred years.

Jihad has been practiced somewhere in the world in every age since the time of the Prophet, and it is firmly based on his teachings in the *Koran*. Orthodox Islam believes that to achieve cosmic order, destroying the earth is acceptable and individual martyrdom is glorious. Allah wills violence in order to redeem mankind.

Al Qaeda and virtually every other "extremist" Islamic group believes that terrorism is firmly based on the teachings of the Koran: Islam requires the mass destruction of not only infidels, but of deviant Muslims as well. "Sacrifice operatives," Al Qaeda's term for suicide bombers, are merely carrying out Mohammed's policies and Allah's will.

A large number of dateable Islamic apocalyptic predictions are still in existence, and all of them agree that early Muslims expected the world to come to an end in the year 717 C.E. The power of apocalyptic belief lies in the fact that these predictions are still readily available in great quantities long after the original predictions were made and demonstrates how important it is to Muslims to force the apocalypse into existence.

Fighting, for Islam, is a proclamation of the faith and a means by which the individual believer is redeemed.

> Yazi b. Sharjara said: "Swords are the keys to paradise; when a man advances upon the enemy, the angels say: "O God, help him!" and when he retreats, they say: "O God, forgive him!" The first drop of blood dripping from the sword brings forgiveness with it for every sin . . ."

In Islam, *jihad* has always been the way to salvation, and this belief has bound disparate Muslim groups together for ages. The concept of jihad has always been the motive behind Islamic conquests, and these conquests are always intended to bring about the apocalypse. Given the history of *jihad* in Islam, it should not be surprising that there is now a resurgence of the practice in our own times.

Islamic literature makes it clear that the *End* means the end of all non-Muslims. Numerous Muslim texts insist that followers of *Allah* must, and will, exterminate all Jews and Christians and establish complete Muslim rule over all the Earth. Non-Muslims have only one choice: convert to Islam or die.

The *Mahdi*, the ninth and last imam, is the expected Messiah of *Shiite* Islam, and it is said that he will be a descendant of Mohammed himself, taking on the name of Mohammed bin Abdullah. The *Mahdi* is expected to be a great spiritual, political and military leader who will emerge after a period of great suffering on Earth. When he arrives, he will lead a revolution and become the Caliph and Imam of all Muslims, creating a new world order and eliminating all those who oppose him.

According to Shiite traditions, the *Mahdi* will invade many countries and will conquer Israel for Islam once and for all. It is written that he will lead a final battle of the faithful in a final slaughter of Jews, and will establish his rule in Jerusalem, from which he will rule over the entire world.

Islam's hatred of Judaism is not a modern development, but dates back to the origins of Islam itself. The mission to annihilate all Jews comes from a curse against Jews in the *Koran* (2:61, and 3:112.) The latter verse is included in Hamas' foundational covenant, along with verses 5:60 and 5:78, which describes Jews as apes and pigs.

The origin of Jewish/Arabic animosity can be traced back to the *Bible* itself. It is first found in the *Genesis* story about Abraham and his two sons, Isaac and Ishmael. Abraham is considered the founding father of both Jewish and Arabic peoples, but Jews are decendants of Isaac and Arabic peoples are decendants of Ishmael. The story of Isaac and Ishmael makes it clear that the enmity between these two Semitic races has continued for a very long time.

In the *Genesis* myth, Abraham is unable to have a son by his wife, Sarah, so Sarah suggests to him that he should sleep with their female slave, Hagar—an Egyptian, so ethnically Arabic. When Hagar conceived Ishmael, she looked upon Sarah with contempt, and this led to her banishment from the household. Many years later Sarah, who was then in her nineties, finally bore a son for Abraham, and called him Isaac.

Both Jews and Muslims agree that the Jewish race descended from Isaac, and the Arabic race descended from Ishmael. In the Genesis story, Ishmael is described as "a wild ass of a man, his hand against every man and every man's hand against him." A further slur against Arabs by Jews was the biblical implication that Hagar was no more than a whore, and Ishmael was not truly legitimate.

If we look closely at the early days of Arabic/Israelite/Christian history we will discover that all three religions persecuted each other at one time or another. When it comes to historical tensions in the Middle East, Jews, Muslims and Christians all have to share some of the blame.

For Shiite Muslims, when the *Madhi* arrives to conquer the world, he will ride a white horse and discover previously unknown biblical manuscripts. It is also predicted that he will even find the original Ark of the Covenant.

The *Mahdi's* power will be of a supernatural nature, since he will receive authority and power directly from Allah—power that will give him dominion even over the wind, rain and crops.

Like Jews and Christians, Muslims believe in a Day of Resurrection, which Muslims call *Yawm al-Qiyamah*, and a Day of

Judgment. This final judgment will result in the annihilation of all of Earth's creatures, even as all human beings will be tested by Allah.

Major and minor signs that will take place before *Aiyamah* (doomsday) comes include:

1. Those who have done good deeds in life will be rewarded, and those who have not will be punished by Allah. The righteous will go to *Jnnat*—heaven—which is a state of bliss. Sinners will be cast into *Jahannam*—a state of extreme suffering. Those who are left on Earth after the Judgment will no longer be subject to death, and those who have been cast into hell at least have the opportunity to purify themselves there and eventually attain heaven.

2. As Christianity predicts the coming of the anti-Christ, Islam predicts the coming of the false messiah, *Al-Maseeh-ud-Dajjal*. *Ad-Dajjal* is supposed to be a great beast-like creature who claims to hold the keys to heaven and hell. Like the anti-Christ, he will lead many people astray, but only unbelievers will be deceived by this beast.

   The false messiah is to have only one good eye, and one blind eye. Like the mark of the beast in *Revelation*, Ad-Dajjal will bear the mark of *Kafir*, the mark of one who does not believe. Also like the anti-Christ, Ad-Dajjal will perform miracles, but only for the purpose of deceiving people. In order to stop Ad-Dajjal, Allah will send Isa—Jesus—to engage Ad-Dajjal in a battle—a battle which Isa will win.

3. Another sign of the coming end of the world will be the appearance of *Ya'jooj* and *Ma'jooj*, two huge tribes of vicious beings which heretofore had been in hiding. So great will be their

power that they will break through the barrier that Allah created to hold them back. Once free, they will ravage the earth. These evil tribes will commit great sins, drink all the water on Earth and destroy plants and animals alike. In the end, however, Allah will send a worm or insect that will wipe out these tribes.

4. The Islamic "new world" will be entirely populated by Muslims, so the extermination of all believers is Islam's "final solution."

XIV. Greek, Roman and Gnostic Eschatology

Traces of eschatological writing can be found in early Greek texts that are far older than *The Bible*. The idea of Hades was not the exclusive invention of Judeo-Christianity, but was common to all Mediterranean peoples; likewise, the belief in an immortal soul. This belief is common among modern Christians, and yet it is heretical. Christian dogma, as recorded in all official Christian creeds, plainly states that the soul does not exist apart from the physical body. After death it remains buried in the ground along with the putrefied flesh. Only when the "general resurrection" occurs is the soul free, and only then as part of the physical body. The ancient Greek understanding of the soul has much more in common with Hinduism than with Christianity.

Greek philosophy allowed for the notion of a final judgment of one's life at the time of death. The deceased—which still contains the aggregates of the immortal soul—awaits judgment and must cross over the river Styx on a ferry conducted by the boatman, Charon. The deceased then stands before a court and awaits judgment. Those guilty of numerous offenses will be sent down the road to the left, which leads to *Tartarus*, a place of punishment. The pious are led down the road on the right, to the Elysian Fields where all is bright and beautiful.

During the Roman period, the mystery religion of Mithraism became popular throughout the Empire. It was contemporary with Christianity. To stamp it out, Hellenistic Christians co-opted its celebratory dates and religious rites. December 25th, for instance, was the birth date of Mithras, so Christians simply appropriated it for the birth date of Jesus.

Other similarities between the two mystery religions (for that is what Christianity really is) are notable. Both religions practiced baptism. Sunday was considered a holy day. Both religions had a Eucharistic meal in which the blood of their god was sanctified. Both religions taught there was a mediator between God and man. Both religions believed in the resurrection of the dead.

Mithraism was directly influenced by Zoroastrianism, and adopted from it the whole notion of a battle between good and evil, a final judgment, the descent of the god to lead a final battle between good and evil. As with all other religions, Mithraism believed there would be a final battle between the forces of light and the forces of darkness.

In Gnosticism, the human condition was considered to be one of ignorance (of our true divine nature) not sin. Acquiring spiritual knowledge, or gnosis, of our true nature was salvation itself. One's true home was the *Pleroma*, the fullness of God, in which all beings dwell. The physical body was conceived of as a prison from which one had to escape in order for the soul to be released and return to the All.

Gnostic Christian eschatology was the reverse of orthodox eschatology. Gnostic Christians (and Jesus himself) believed that the kingdom of God was a present reality, not some event that would take place in the future. The kingdom was already present, and one could enter it simply by recognizing its existence.

Gnostics were aware that the world (planet Earth) would end one day, but instead of emphasizing future events that would take place in the distant future, they believed in what scholars call "realized eschatology." The practical and personal "end of the world" would take place when each individual overcame human ignorance. Anyone who achieved personal illumination—true gnosis—would at that moment be "saved." Being "alive in Christ" meant that the Gnostic had already achieved immortality.

Once the principals for dispelling inner darkness were learned, the successful Gnostic lived in a state of grace from that moment forward. When the physical body died, matter would return to matter, and spirit would return to Spirit.

"Realized eschatology" was not a late Christian heresy, but existed from the beginning. The proof can be found in Paul's first letter to his church in Corinth. In Paul's absence, more than a few members of that congregation had accepted the Gnostic definition of "resurrection" as something that could be achieved while one was still alive.

Paul angrily chastised these "heretics" because he taught that ultimate salvation and immortality—life in Christ—could be achieved only when the *general resurrection* of the dead took place at the end of time.

XV. 2012 and the Mayan Calendar

Take one quintuplified planetary alignment.
Sprinkle in an always mystifying solar eclipse. Stir
in a potload of craziness—prayer vigils in Bombay,
shelter-stocking in the United States, jittery sky-
gazing everywhere—and you've got yourself an
all-out Apocalypse Watch. Nothing happens, of
course. But the Antichrist was born the next day,
at least according to noted psychic, Jeane Dixon.

- JASON BOYETT

B y now I hope that I have made a sufficient case demon-
strating that Jewish and Christian apocalypses were not
meant to be predictions of the distant future. Yet, such
predictions—since they seem common to humanity as a whole—
certainly seem to apply to our present times. If every religion has
had premonitions about the end of life as we know it, perhaps we
should pay attention.

What, then, to make of the supposed predictions of the Maya
that the world as we know it will end in 2012? I'll make my own
prediction: On December 21st, 2012, the day on which the world
as we know it will end according to "authorities" such as Jose'
Arguelles, nothing dramatic is going to happen. But that date is
as good as any other to mark a turning point for humanity. If the
end is already under way then the world is only going to be much

worse off by the end of 2012.

But the New Age movement looks to this date, not so much in terms of "the end," but a date signifying the beginning of a major change in human consciousness. While I am skeptical, I still hope they are right.

Jose' Arguelles is the best known proponent of the Mayan Calendar myth, but he has a history of making predictions that do not come true. Arguelles originally predicted that the world would end August 16-17, 1987 in an event he called "Harmonic Convergence." He based this prediction on the Mayan calendar as well, but 1987 came and went and the world did not end.

This time Arguelles has gone farther out on a limb by stating that there will be a quantum leap in human consciousness after the events that take place on December 21st, 2012. According to Arguelles and the New Age Movement, human consciousness will expand exponentially after December 21, 2012. Back in the 1960s and early 1970s, the Counter Culture believed the same thing. It announced that we were entering the Age of Aquarius: "When the moon is in the seventh House, and Jupiter aligns with Mars, then peace will guide the planets and love will steer the stars." It was a nice sentiment, and I believed it. But it turned out to be little more than wishful thinking.

Arguelles has many critics. He is an intelligent man who holds a PhD, but actual Mayan scholars and archaeologists don't interpret the Mayan calendar the way he does. Some scholars even claim that Arguelles didn't do his math correctly. Critics argue that Arguelles' calculations are based on a different day-count than actually exists in the Mayan calendar. According to the traditional count, the world should have ended January 1, 2005. Arguelles also claims that his Thirteen Moon Calendar is synchronized with the calendar round, but experts say this is not the case. If the traditional count were used, then the world has already ended.

Supposedly the Mayans were excellent astronomers and

mathematicians, but contrary to popular belief, they did not even create their calendar. They merely extended a calendar system that was already common in Mesoamerican cultures—even though their refinements were quite sophisticated.

But weren't the Mayans those people who practiced human sacrifice, and used the decapitated heads of their enemies as soccer balls? And did not the Mayans bring about their own apocalypse? UCLA professor, Jared Diamond, in his book, *Collapse: How Societies Choose to Fail or Succeed*, argues that the Mayans became extinct due to greed, constant warfare and environmental destruction. They are hardly our best role models.

In Mayan lore, the people acquired their calendar from their deity, Itzamna, who was considered the founder of Mayan culture. The Mayan sense of time was both linear and cyclical. Mixing mathematics, astronomy and superstition, the Mayans believed that each cycle of time (called a *baktun*) had its own special character.

Mayan events and ritual ceremonies coincided with auspicious dates. In predicting the future, Mayan priests proposed that future occurrences would be subject to the same influences upon them as during previous cycles. Their particular theory of cycles was projected on observable phenomena, and yet they failed to learn from their mistakes.

The Mayan Sacred Round, called the *Tzolk'in* made up a 260-day calendar, and the *Habb'* was a solar calendar made up of eighteen months of twenty days, including five nameless days at the end of the year known as *Wayeb'*. The *Haab'* was first used around 550 BC. with the winter solstice being the starting point.

As a calendar for keeping track of the seasons, the *Haab'* was a bit inaccurate, since it treated the year as having exactly 365 days, and ignored the extra quarter day in the actual tropical year. This meant that over a period of several centuries the calendar became less and less accurate. The *Haab'* is equivalent to the wandering 365-day year of the ancient Egyptians.

The five nameless days at the end of the calendar, called the *Wayeb'*, were thought to be a dangerous time when portals between the mortal realm and the Underworld dissolved. On these days, there were no defenses to prevent the appearance of deities intent on causing disasters. Prudent Mayans avoided leaving their houses during those days when evil spirits might be present.

For the Mayans, the apocalypse arrived all too soon. Too bad they failed to predict it.

XVI. Hindu Eschatology
The Kali Yuga

*Social status depends not upon your accomplishments,
but in the ownership of property; wealth is now the only
source of virtue; passion and luxury are the sole bonds
between spouses; falsity and lying are the conditions of
success in life; sexuality is the sole source of human
enjoyment; religion, a superficial and empty ritual,
is confused with spirituality.*

- *THE VISHNU PURANA* (100 BCE)

According to Hindus, a *Yuga* is an epoch or era within a cycle of four ages. These are the *Satya Yuga* (or *Krita Yuga*), the *Treta Yuga*, the *Dvapara Yuga* and finally the Kali Yuga. We are now living in the Kali Yuga, named after Kali, the goddess of destruction.

According to Hindu cosmology, life in the universe is created and destroyed once every 4.11 to 8.2 billion years, which is one full day and night of *Brahma* (God the creator). In the cyclical system of creation and destruction, the fourth cycle—the Kali Yuga—is the age in which Homo sapiens first appeared. This seems to suggest that the human race was destined to fail right from the beginning.

The fourth age is ruled over by Kali, goddess of destruction, who is the consort of *Shiva*, god of destruction—the third member of the triune godhead: *Brahman*. In this trinity, *Brahma* is the creator, *Vishnu*, the sustainer of creation, and *Shiva* inevitably destroys all that has been created. Shiva's cosmic dance of destruction is not a negative image, however. Shiva destroys whenever creation has become weary and useless so that creation can begin all over again. On a cosmic scale, the cycles of creation and destruction of worlds and universes are repeated endlessly throughout all eternity.

It is predicted that in the Kali Yuga, nobility in human society will be predicated upon the amount of wealth one acquires. One's place of birth, and even a lifetime of virtuous behavior are of no consequence. Brute force is the order of the day and the standard for deciding what is righteous or just. Greed, graft and corruption are the accepted norms in business, and an individual's worth is based solely on his or her wealth and the ability to sexually gratify another.

In the Kali Yuga, of the four pillars of the *Dharma* (spiritual teachings/spiritual path), charity is all that remains of penance, truthfulness, compassion and charity. But it, too, decreases daily. Unrighteousness increases at the same rate. When all the forces of destruction combine, they will cause human societies and the life force of the planet to collapse. When this happens, the *Dharma* will become extinct.

At the true end of the world, and the dissolution of this Universe, Shiva will appear to defeat the greatest demon of the age and perform the Dance of Tandava on his back. This mystical dance is considered to be the greatest of all martial arts and it will destroy all forms of matter and energy. Upon destruction everything will be reabsorbed into *Brahman*, the One who alone exists.

On Earth, the final avatar, Kalki, will appear at the end of the Kali Yuga and wage a final battle between good and evil. Kalki will ride a white horse and amass an army of those few pious souls remaining. These, together with all the incarnations of the

Godhead (avatars) which have appeared throughout human history, will destroy all demons and sins in the world.

According to the *Vedic* tradition of Hinduism, *Aditi* is mother of eight *Adityas* or solar deities. At the end of creation these eight suns will shine together in the skies.

In Earth history, the avatar, Kalki, will reestablish righteousness upon Earth; and the minds of those who live at the end of the Kali age will become enlightened and their minds will be filled with clarity. Those who are transformed by virtue will be the new seeds of a higher form of humanity. These men and women will give birth to a race of humans who will follow the laws of a new beginning, and the Krita Yuga will begin again. It is said: "When the sun and moon, the lunar constellation, *Tishya,* and the planet Jupiter are all in one mansion, the Krita age shall return to Earth."

A bleaker scenario is suggested in the *Vishnu Puranas*. In this text, at the end of human history there will be an ever greater increase in unemployment, arrogance, dishonesty, greed, lack of discipline, false messiahs and religions, evil rulers, moral perversion, abortion, and lust for power. Earth will be valued only for her mineral treasures, and only those without wealth will exhibit honesty. Men with many faults, who merely exhibit a pretense of greatness, will rule human societies. Humanity will be plagued with fatal diseases, famine, drought and human misery of all kinds. Those who survive will do so only in the wilderness, once again living off of nature. And in the end, humankind will be completely destroyed.

XVII. Seven Suns: The Buddha's Discourse on the End of the World

The religion of the future will be a cosmic religion.
It should transcend personal God and avoid dogma
and theology. Covering both the natural and the
spiritual, it should be based on a religious sense arising
from the experience of all things natural and spiritual as
a meaningful unity. Buddhism answers this description.
If there is any religion that could cope with modern
scientific needs it would be Buddhism.

-ALBERT EINSTEIN

It is said that the Buddha himself claimed that his teachings would eventually disappear after five thousand years, and so would all the moral concepts he taught. Even the Dharma—the teachings and the path—will cease to be. There will be a new era when the next Buddha Maitreya will appear, but it will be preceded by the degeneration of human society. This will be a period of greed, lust, poverty, ill will, violence, murder, impiety, physical weakness, sexual depravity and general societal collapse. Even the Buddha himself will be forgotten.

The Buddha's elaboration on the theme of how seven suns will appear in the sky before Earth is destroyed, is a progression of seven steps.

When the first sun appears, the Earth will suffer from extreme drought. All vegetation on Earth with disappear. When the second sun appears, streams and ponds will dry up. When the third sun appears, even the mighty Ganges will dry up.

After a long period of time, a fourth sun will appear, and the great lakes will evaporate. Much later, a fifth sun will appear and the oceans will slowly dry up. Many more years will pass until a sixth sun appears, and the Earth itself will start to burn. Volcanoes will explode, the Earth will become scorched, and the skies will be full of smoke.

After another great span of time, a seventh sun will appear and the Earth itself will become a ball of fire. It will expand and finally explode and disappear forever.

It seems amazing that the Buddha predictions of the end of planet Earth so closely match those of modern astronomers.

The Blessed One addressed the monks and spoke of the end of the world, saying,

> All things are impermanent, all aspects of existence are unstable and non-eternal. Beings will become so weary and disgusted with the constituent things that they will seek emancipation from them more quickly.

> There will come a season, O monks when, after hundreds of thousands of years, rains will cease. All seedlings, all vegetation, all plants, grasses and trees will dry up and cease to be. Thus it is that all constituent things are impermanent, unstable, non-eternal. This will make one so weary he will seek emancipation from all of these.

> There comes another season after a great lapse of time when a second sun will appear. Now all brooks and

ponds will dry up, vanish, cease to be. And so, all constituent things are impermanent. Then after another
vast interval a third sun will appear, and all the great
rivers, the Ganges, the *Jamna*, the *Rapti*, the *Gorgra*, the
Hahi will dry up, vanish and cease to be.

Again after a vast period of time a fourth sun will appear and the great lakes—the *Anotatto*, the Lion-leap,
Chariot-maker, *Keel-bare*, Cuckoo, Six-bayed and Slow-
flow will dry up and cease to be.

Again, monks, after another long period a fifth sun
will appear and the waters of the great oceans will
be reduced a hundred leagues, then two hundred,
three hundred, even to seven hundred leagues will
the oceans be reduced until they are waste deep, knee
deep, ankle-deep. After the appearance of the fifth sun,
the oceans will be reduced to finger deep.

Again after a vast period of time a sixth sun will appear, and it will bake the Earth even as a pot is baked
by a potter. All the mountains will reek and send up
clouds of smoke.

After another great interval a seventh sun will appear
and the Earth will blaze with fire until it becomes one
mass of flame. The mountains will be consumed, a
spark will be carried on the wind and go to the worlds
of God. The peaks of Mount Sineru will burn, will be
consumed, will perish, and will crumble in a mass of
fire. Not even ashes will remain.

Thus, O monks are the constituent things of existence unstable, non-eternal. And this alone is enough to make one weary, to become disgusted with constituent things until they are emancipated. Thus, monks, all things will burn, perish and exist no more except those who have seen the path.

FROM *THE PALI CANON*

As in Hinduism, Buddhism believes that Earth's history progresses in cycles. In this regard, human nature was not set in the beginning, but became subject to these cycles, or *suttas*. Once humans lived for an immensely long time, even 80,000 years, and they were beautiful, wealthy, and had great pleasure and strength.

Over time, however, humanity lost its ability to live skillfully until one's life-span is reduced to a hundred years. All beauty, wealth, pleasure and strength are reduced accordingly.

In future times, morality will decline and the human life-span will be reduced until it becomes ten years, and sexual maturity will be reached at five years. As human life deteriorates further, humans will take up swords and hunt one another as if they were game animals. Some people will escape the slaughter by taking shelter in the wilderness. When the time of killing ends, they will come out, and humans will once more be virtuous. Again the human life-span will increase, and sexual maturity will not be reached until the age of 500.

In other Buddhist traditions, before the world is destroyed by fire, "shining ones"—light beings—will appear and announce the end of the world. They will urge people to practice loving-kindness, compassion, sympathetic joy and equanimity.

When the rain stops and plants dry up there is famine among humanity. Beings from hell escape and are reborn in the human world, but will make a gradual progression upward until they are reborn in the Brahma (God) world. Those with seriously bad karma will be reborn in "unfortunate destinations."

In the *Kalachakra Tantra* of Tibetan Buddhism, we find the concept of Buddhist holy war against Islam, using the same names and images found in the Hindu *Vishnu Purana*. Non-Indic people (Muslims) will come to rule physical India and the symbolic land of *Shambhala* in the year 2424 C.E. There will be a final war between good and evil, with Islam being part of that evil.

There will be battles between *Krinmati*, the twelfth *Mahdi*, and *Raudrachakrin*, the 25th Kalki, who will invade India and defeat the Muslims who have temporarily conquered that land. This apocalyptic battle will mark the end of the Kali Yuga, and the beginning of a new golden age. Buddhists who allegorize this text still make an anti-Muslim statement: "Mohammed" represents "the pathway of destructive behavior." The horse on which the Islamic *Mahdi* rides symbolizes unawareness of behavioral cause and effect. The *Mahdi's* four army divisions represent hatred, malice, resentment and prejudice, the exact opposites of the armed forces of *Shambhala*. Raudrachakrin's victory represents the attainment of the path to liberation and enlightenment.

XVIII. Native American Prophecies

Only after the last tree has been cut down,
Only after the last river has been poisoned,
Only after the last fish has been caught,
Only then will you find that money cannot be eaten.

- CREE INDIAN PROPHECY

Hopi Prophecy

Hopi prophecy predicts that World War III will be started by people who received the Light—China, Palestine, India and Africa. When the war comes, America will be destroyed by "gourds of ashes" which will fall to the ground. The rivers will boil and the Earth will burn. There will be diseases which have no cures. Turtle Island (America) will turn over and the oceans will meet the sky. When the *Saquahuh* (blue Star) Kachina dances in the plaza and removes his mask, the times of trial will have begun, and only the Hopi will be saved.

The Hopi, White Feather, predicted that the fourth world would end soon, and the fifth will begin. The first sign will be the coming of the white man who steals the land that is not his. They will strike their enemies with thunder (guns?) .

The second sign will be the coming of spinning wheels filled with voices (wagon trains?). The third sign will be a strange beast like a buffalo, with great long horns (long horn cattle?) and these will overrun the land in large numbers.

The fourth sign will be the land crossed by snakes of iron (railroad tracks?). The fifth sign is a land criss-crossed by a giant spider's web (telephone and electrical wires?). The sixth sign will be the land criss-crossed with rivers of stone that make pictures in the sun (concrete highways with their mirage-producing effects?). The seventh sign will be the sea turning black, and many living things dying because of it (oil spills?) The eighth sign will be many youth who wear their hair long and join the tribal nations to learn their wisdom (the hippies of the 1960s?). The ninth and last sign will be a blue dwelling place in the skies that will fall with a great crash (The U.S. Space Station, Skylab, which fell to Earth in 1979?). Witnesses at the time remarked that it appeared to be burning blue.

White man will battle against all other peoples on the Earth, especially those who possessed the first light of wisdom. But in the end, the *Pahana* or "True White Brother" will return to plant the seeds of wisdom in people's hearts, and thus usher in the dawn of the Fifth World.

Sioux Prophecy

According to an Ogalala medicine man, darkness will descend and the world will become out of balance. There will be floods, fires and earthquakes. White Buffalo Calf Woman will then purify the world. She will bring back harmony and spiritual balance.

Cherokee Prophecy

The Cherokee Nation Calendar is written in the Star Constellation, Rattlesnake, which is the prophecy of "Time/Un-time." The Serpent will take on head feathers, its eyes will open and glow, it wings will spring forth. It will develop arms and legs, and its hands will hold a bowl of blood.

Cherokee tradition, like so many other cultures, retains the myth of the Tree of Life, with its roots buried far into earth and its branches spreading themselves into the sky. For the Cherokee, the Tree of Life symbolizes rebirth and renewal. The Cherokee calendar ends in the year 2012!

Another Cherokee story foretells a monster with white eyes. This evil monster will cross the seas and with its terrifying power it will destroy everything in its path. The animals and trees, along with their spirits will begin to die. Mother Earth will be torn asunder and its heartbeat will become faint. The monster will consume all of the children of Turtle Island. But in the end the white-eyed monster will be overcome and everyone will live in peace. Trees and animals will be safe once more, and the monster will cease to exist.

Cree Prophecy

During the nineteenth century an old Cree wise woman named "Eyes of Fire" prophesied that one day white man will blacken the waters, poison fish, destroy all forests and cause birds to fall from the sky. When all of this has come to pass, Rainbow Warriors will appear in order to restore balance. After the Warriors have done their cleansing work, all the tribes of the Earth will form a new world of justice, peace and freedom. Then all human beings will finally recognize the existence of the Great Spirit.

These Warriors will teach others the true principles for living on the Earth. They will teach us how to live in harmony with all peoples. In the new world we will all learn to love the Earth and, because of this, will once again feel joy. We will be free of petty jealousies and our love of all people will transcend race and religion.

Our minds, hearts, souls and deeds will be filled with pure thoughts, and we will seek the beauty of the Great Spirit. Children will once again be able to run free and enjoy the treasures of nature—free from the fears of toxins and destruction brought about by white man's greed. The rivers will once again run clear. Forests will return and be abundant. Animals will return and be respected. The poor, sick and those in need will be cared for by their brothers and sisters. New leaders will be chosen for the quality of their character, not for their power and wealth.

The Rainbow Warriors will face many and great challenges. There will be great mountains of ignorance, prejudice and hatred to overcome. Thus, they must be dedicated, unwavering in their strength and strong of heart. This day will come, and it is not far away.

XIX. The Human Stain

Hell is empty; all the demons are here.

- SHAKESPEARE, *THE TEMPEST*

We have come to the brink of destruction today due to the choices we have made over a period of thousands of years. Based on greed and selfishness, these choices have made us a "Human Stain" upon the Earth as novelist, Philip Ross put it. This stain has dyed the entire world black.

Anthropologists once believed that our ancestor, Homo neanderthalensis, became extinct before Homo sapiens came along. Now there is positive proof that these two hominid groups actually existed side by side for at least 5,000 years. Both species learned how to make fire, basic tools and weapons. And while there is no absolute proof of this, it seems likely that both species competed against each other for the same resources.

Then, quite suddenly, Neanderthals ceased to exist. Were we responsible for the extinction of this hominid species, as we were in the case of the wooly mammoth and saber toothed tiger? Could the myth of Cain killing Abel be a metaphor for what Homo sapiens did to Homo neanderthalensis? We may never know for sure, but we do know that Homo sapiens is an unrivaled killing machine—the most dangerous animal to ever walk the planet.

In the beginning we lived in harmony with nature, just as aboriginal peoples have done throughout human history. But then something in our nature changed. Did we change with malice aforethought, or were we merely victims of evolution?

Whatever the case, we took a fork in the road that has led straight to the apocalypse. Not only did we learn murder along the way, but we came to view nature as nothing more than a collection of "resources." Many of us believe that other life forms on the planet have no intrinsic value—no right to exist for their own sake. If we do not change this attitude, our greed and selfishness will lead to the extinction of *all* life on the planet. And if nature ceases to exist, we will cease to exist.

We understood this in the beginning, but evolution transformed us from hunter-gathers into agriculturists and slaughterers of animals. Once humanity believed it needed land in order to cultivate crops and feed animals, we had to acquire land by whatever means necessary, including war.

This arrogance of man is represented in the *Bible*—especially in the *Book of Joshua*. This biblical book tells us that the Israelites "massacred" the Canaanites—the original residents of the "promised land." The Hebrew tribes had gradually become an agrarian people and needed land on which to farm. The Canaanites, by contrast, were town dwellers and pastoral; they raised animals, not crops, and they were still hunter-gathers in large measure. Once again, Cain killed Abel.

In order to capture the land of Canaan and surrounding territories the Israelites, by their own admission, practiced ethnic cleansing. Beginning in the book of *Exodus*, God tells his "chosen people" that He will give them "a good and spacious land, flowing with milk and honey." In order to accomplish this, Yahweh commands, "Of the cities . . . . which the Lord thy God gave thee for an inheritance, thou shalt save alive nothing that breatheth." (*Deuteronomy* 20:16)

At Jericho, "They [the Israelites] utterly destroyed men, women, young and old, oxen, sheep and asses, with the edge of the sword" (*Joshua* 6:21). "They slaughtered all the inhabitants of Ai" (*Joshua* 8:24). And in Hazor "They did not leave any that breathed" (*Joshua* 11: 20). The enemy in Goshen "should be utterly destroyed, and should receive no mercy, but be *exterminated*" (*Joshua* 11:20).

Just like individuals, every nation has its own karma based on all the actions it has taken throughout its history. The United States is now reaping its karma for stealing this land and decimating the indigenous peoples to whom it originally belonged.

Ancient Israel's karma for stealing the land of Canaanites was in being conquered themselves. Today, Israel is once again surrounded by enemies who are intent on its destruction for precisely the same reason: the theft of land.

Unless there is a change of heart and policy in modern Israel, the Middle East may very well become the actual scene of the mythical battle of Armageddon. Christian fundamentalists hope this war will take place because they believe it will signal the beginning of the Apocalypse. They very well may get their wish.

Even if we do not annihilate ourselves with nuclear weapons, we can easily end the world by consuming all of its remaining resources—an inevitability unless we can reverse population growth. As a species, we must wake up from the nightmare we have inflicted upon ourselves. But this is God's last offer: change, or face the fires of our own self-made hell.

XX. Modern Post-Apocalyptic and Dystopian Views of the Future

Wild, dark times are rumbling toward us, and the prophet who wishes to write a new apocalypse will have to invent entirely new beasts, and beasts so terrible that the ancient animal symbols of St. John will seem like cooing doves and cupids in comparison.

- HEINRICH HEINE—1843

One half of all the forests that existed 8,000 years ago no longer exist. Half of this loss has taken place in the past fifty years. We are supposed to be a paperless society, yet paper consumption has increased five-fold over the past two decades. Most distressing of all: only 12% of the remaining forests lie within protected lands.

During the 1960s I read the book, *The Population Bomb*, by Paul R. Ehrlich. I was shocked at what I read. Human population had doubled in the past thirty years to three billion people. Ehrlich predicted that it would double again by 1990 if we did nothing about the problem. We did nothing and the population did double. Now there are more than six billion people on the planet. If we continue to do nothing, it will double again in another twenty years.

Having too many people on the planet, using up too many resources, has led to global warming, deforestation, destruction

of food chains, and dying oceans. Besides being nearly fished out, half of all the coral reefs in the oceans of the world are already gone, and half of what remains will be lost by 2030.

The Earth is losing biodiversity as the result of a mass extinction of species. Food chains are being destroyed, wetlands are disappearing, and our rivers and streams are impaired. We have to deal with toxic waste, water unfit to drink and air unfit to breathe. The introduction of alien species of plants and animals to pristine natural environments is causing all kinds of havoc as well.

In human society, indigenous peoples are disappearing. Mass starvation in the world's poorest nations has become the rule, not the exception. The world is faced with terrorism, political unrest, political murders, political corruption, civil wars, war lords, militias, genocide, ethnic cleansing, pandemics and the possibility of nuclear war.

How is it that we can ignore all this? For Americans, the answer is simple: supermarket shelves are full, grass is still green, and the sky—at least in most places—is still blue. We have learned to get along with bottled water—even if it does come in non-biodegradable plastic. In short, most of us, most of the time, don't see evidence suggesting that society is about to collapse.

In spite of present economic problems, things seem fine in First World nations. But this is only because we have stolen the rest of the world's resources. Eighty percent of humanity lives in poverty, and half of those are on the brink of starvation. Yet, we are rarely reminded of this on the evening news, and if we don't see the problems it's easy to believe they don't exist.

Many people believe that technology will save us, yet technology—and the age of industrialization before it—is the source of most of our problems to begin with. Better health care, for instance, has resulted in over population which, in turn, has led to environmental destruction.

Ease and convenience of travel have led to dependence on

non-renewable energy sources, which have led to wars, which have led to environmental destruction. Bionics is helping improve the lives of people missing arms and legs, and that is leading to the merging of man with machine. Once our brains have been downloaded to machines, we will live forever—as cyborgs. No matter; in the post-human future we will have hybrid pets and grow furniture in fields. We call this "progress."

Computers and the Internet have given us wonderful opportunities, but have also led to our loss of privacy. Dependence on computers has made our entire nation vulnerable to hackers and all manner of computer viruses. Worse still, electromagnetic pulse bombs actually exist, and if they are deployed and explode over our cities, virtually all electronics will cease to function. We won't be able to communicate. We won't even be able to start our cars. Nearly all technological achievements also have a downside.

Then there is the political and financial struggle for world domination; country against country, special interest against special interest—everyone seeking control over the masses. In his book, *1984*, written in 1949, George Orwell imagined our future in a police-state. Orwell may have gotten the date wrong, but many of his other predictions have proven accurate. Just as the novel predicted, we have developed "doublespeak" and "newspeak." Our military calls a missile built to kill people, a "peacemaker." Suspects are "persons of interest." Our government no longer lies; it just spreads "disinformation."

We don't forget anymore, we just "misremember." When we speak, we must be "politically correct." If not, we are guilty of "thought crimes." If we dare to speak out against anything at all, we are directed to "free speech zones." At the moment, our country is waging two wars, but we don't see the carnage because television cameras are no longer allowed on the battlefield. We are told what to believe and we believe it.

In 1949, Aldous Huxley wrote George Orwell to congratulate him on his book. He predicted:

> Within the next generation I believe that the world's leaders will discover that infant conditioning and nar-co-hypnosis are more efficient, as instruments of government, than clubs and prison, and that the lust for power can be just as completely satisfied by suggesting people into loving their servitude as by flogging them and kicking them into obedience.

If we wish to use the airlines we must utterly submit to authority no matter how absurd its demands. We are forced to half undress, and x-rays can now scan our naked bodies. We dare not protest. We dare not joke. One wrong word and we can be made to "disappear."

We lost our right to due process of the law when the Patriot Act was passed after 9/11. Now we can disappear or be locked up without ever being charged with a crime, without ever being informed of our rights, and without being allowed to have a lawyer. We might imagine a 1984 nightmare taking place in Russia, China, North Korea, Miramar, Iran and a host of banana republics, but we do not expect it here. Yet it is happening here, and there is hardly a whisper of protest. But don't worry about any of this because our government tells us it has our best interests at heart.

We should be grateful that Big Brother is watching us. Thanks to the World Wide Web, now anybody can gain access to our vital records, and even steal our identity. Any arm of the government can track us at any time because our physical location can be triangulated through our cell phones.

Cameras in orbit take pictures of our houses. There are cameras watching us in airports, in stores, on highways, and even in parks and on beaches. The government wants to embed electronic chips into the flesh of children so that they can be traced if they are

ever kidnapped. So children with chips in their arms will grow up to be adults with chips in their arms. Big Brother will then be able to track everyone everywhere—for our own protection.

Because we don't have enough prisons to accommodate our growing class of criminals, prisoners in various parts of the country are being released back into society wearing devices that allow them to be tracked, monitored and rearrested in an instant. Implants are being developed for psychopaths and child molesters that will allow law enforcement to monitor peoples moods and every glitch in their thought processes. This will allow us to prevent crime by arresting people before they commit a crime. We will soon be able to arrest felons for merely having the intention of committing a crime. Thought crimes will be punishable to the full extent of the law, so don't even think about it.

Many of the predictions in Aldous Huxley's book, *Brave New World*—written in 1932—have also become reality. Making babies and giving birth no longer have to be natural acts. Embryos can be frozen. Embryos can be grown in test tubes. Natural birth and natural parenting are gradually disappearing. Now we have sperm donors and surrogate mothers.

Our food contains pesticides, additives and is genetically manipulated. The rising rate of cancer in America suggests that we are what we eat, and that's not necessarily a good thing. We have square tomatoes, and "Frankenfoods." Scientists are tinkering with our genes to make us healthier, or make us more complacent and compliant. Alphas—the intentionally bred highest cast—already run the world, and Deltas—also known as illegal aliens—already do all the dirty work.

Now we can clone animals, and one day, if it hasn't happened already, we will clone human beings. How long will it be before humans are bred to suit the needs of the state? Even "Soma," the ubiquitous happy pill of Huxley's novel, is now a real drug. It doesn't make anyone happy, but we have other drugs for that. We are medicated and motivated.

Post-apocalyptic films like *Soylent Green*, *Blade Runner*, or *Mad Max* do not seem all that outrageous if we are paying attention to what's going on in the real world. These nightmare scenarios of the future are all too believable. In *Soylent Green*, there are so many people on the planet that food has run out. Suicide is encouraged so that humans can be recycled as food. *Blade Runner's* dystopian world is governed by giant corporations, not governments. In this future, too, there are wall-to-wall people and incentive plans encouraging good citizens to move "off planet."

In the three *Mad Max* movies, the bombs have already fallen and those humans who are left must fight each other like animals just to survive. Though the *Terminator* series of movies showed what will surely happen if we merge man and machine, a recent article in *National Geographic* featured real technology and real companies working night and day to re-create the human race as a society of cyborgs. Keep the brain, replace all the body parts.

Have a nice day.

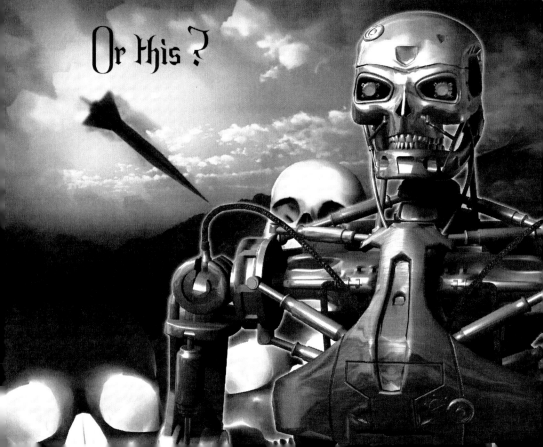

CONCLUSION

Don't blame yourself. The apocalypse wasn't your
fault. Actually, it was just as much your fault as it
was anyone else's. Come to think of it, if you're an
American, it was probably about 80-90% more your
fault than the average human. But don't let that get
you down. It wasn't exclusively your fault. Unless
you're the president. Then it might be your fault.
But you'll have plenty of interns to tell you
that it wasn't, so you'll be fine.

- MEGHANN MARCO

So what conclusions have we come to after studying the apocalyptic traditions presented here? Is Earth going to end some day? That much is certain. Is the world *as we know it* going to end? That is less certain, but in many respects the question comes too late. The world as we have known it is already ending. Clearly, this too is inevitable.

Will the end of the present world lead to a dystopian future, or will it trigger a quantum leap in human consciousness as the New Age Movement believes? I shudder at the former and hope for the latter, but in the end I cannot predict the outcome.

I do know that if we are to survive, survival will come at a price, and it is a very steep price. We must learn to walk lightly on the Earth. This change in thinking about our place in nature, rather than our place above it, will require us all to make great sacrifices. Are we willing to make them?

At the present moment, the collapse of human civilization seems all too possible. This has been predicted, and may be inevitable. But we cannot simply view destruction as something evil and unwanted. The death of the world as we have known it may be necessary for our species to move on to a higher level of consciousness simply by being forced to confront the consequences of our selfishness and greed. In the end, the final battle between good and evil will not take place "out there," but within ourselves.

Nothing new is ever created without the destruction of what came before it. As Jesus pointed out, no one puts new wine in old wineskins, for they will burst. If we are giving birth to a New Age, we cannot expect the birthing process to be painless. The destruction of much of what we love may be the catalyst that forces us to transcend our limited consciousness and create a new world.

In the meantime, what should we do as individuals? We can make all kinds of personal sacrifices that will lighten the load of Mother Nature. We can prepare for our own evolution of consciousness. What we can't do is force the world to change. Taoism questions whether we should even try. Wanting things to be different from what they are is, in many respects, a neurosis of the human mind. We can neither push the river nor reverse its course.

Happiness comes as the result of accepting "reality" for what it is, not in visualizing an idealized future. Wishing for things to be different is a neurosis of the human mind. Utopia truly is "no place."

Working toward creating a better world, however, is not neurotic. It is human nature to seek perfection. We are genetically programmed to challenge the gods, to attempt to defeat the Cherubim, cast away the fiery sword and seize the Tree of Life. Being imperfect divinities ourselves, we will make mistakes along the way. More often than not, we learn from them.

Being created in the image of the gods means we have the power to both create and destroy. We are god-like and demonic in equal measure. But every spiritual master who has ever lived has told us the same thing: we can transcend our dualistic consciousness—this split between our God-self and our shadow—because our essential nature is divine.

What I find most interesting about all apocalyptic predictions is the commonly held belief that a new creation—a new world—will follow the destruction of this world. As a species, we are often greedy, ignorant, selfish and careless, but we have one redeeming quality: optimism. If the world as we know it has to end, so be it. Perhaps all the apocalyptic predictions will turn out to be correct, but we cannot expect That-Which-Is to provide us with a new world—a better world—to take the place of this one.

We can depend only on ourselves. If there is a better world to come, it will be because we created it.

> It shall come to pass at the End of Days that the mountain of the house of the Lord shall be established as the highest of the mountains, and shall be raised above the hills; and the nations shall flow to it, and many people shall come . . .

> and He shall judge between the nations, and shall decide for many people and they shall beat their swords into plowshares, and their spears into pruning hooks; nation shall not lift up sword against nation, neither shall they learn war any more.

> *- ISAIAH 2:2-4*

ABOUT THE AUTHOR

ev. Richard Hooper is a former Lutheran pastor and present Interfaith minister who holds graduate degrees in both theology and the philosophy of world religions. He has been a life-long lay scholar in the areas of the historical Jesus, early Christianity, Gnosticism and world religions. Rev. Hooper is the founder of Sanctuary Publications and The Sedona Institute for Comparative Religion. He is author of:

- *The Crucifixion of Mary Magdalene*
- *The Gospel of the Unknown Jesus*
- *Jesus, Buddha, Krishna, Lao Tzu: The Parallel Teachings*
- *Hymns to the Beloved: the Poetry, Prayers and Wisdom of the World's Great Mystics*
- *The Real Secrets of Christianity* (eBook), and
- *End of Days: Predictions of the End from Ancient Sources.*

Richard Hooper is an associate member of the Jesus Seminar, and member of the Order of Universal Interfaith (OUnI) as well as the Order of the Mystic Heart (OMH).

He lives in Sedona, Arizona with his wife, Sharon.

Priceless treasuries of interfaith understanding by Richard Hooper from Sanctuary Publications

Hymns to the Beloved has been designed as a companion volume to Richard Hooper's previous book, Jesus, Buddha, Krishna, Lao Tzu: the Parallel Sayings. Both are filled with beautiful and inspiring photographs and selected readings and poetry from the world's mystical traditions.

Richard Hooper...blazes a path of collective understanding beyond dogma toward finding the divinity within ourselves.

- Judy Martin, National Radio Journalist

Sanctuary Publications
P. O. Box 20697 • Sedona, AZ 86341
info@SanctuaryPublications.com
www.SanctuaryPublications.com

Hymns
to the
Beloved

The poetry, prayers and wisdom of the world's great mystics

Edited with commentaries by
RICHARD HOOPER

ISBN 13: 978-0-9785334-5-8 • $22.95

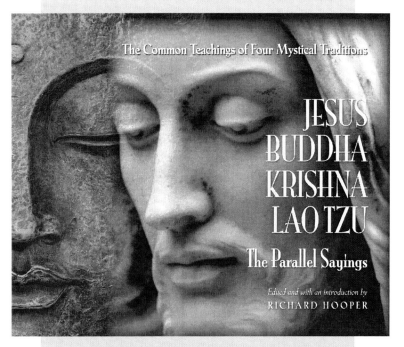

The Common Teachings of Four Mystical Traditions

JESUS
BUDDHA
KRISHNA
LAO TZU

The Parallel Sayings

Edited and with an introduction by
RICHARD HOOPER

ISBN 13: 978-0-9785334-9-6 • $22.95

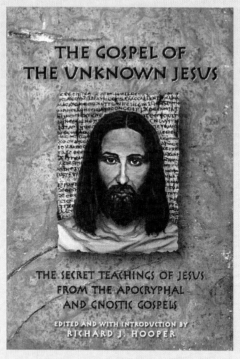

ISBN: 0-9746995-5-1 • $16.95

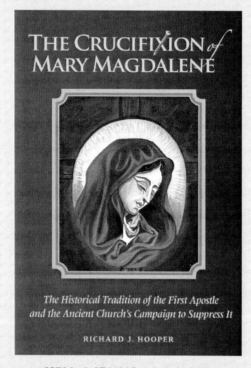

ISBN: 0-9746995-4-3 • $18.95